GHOST WALKS IN
LEICESTERSHIRE

GHOST WALKS IN LEICESTERSHIRE

Barbara Wadd

First published in Great Britain in 2010 by
Derby Books Publishing Company Limited
3 The Parker Centre,
Derby, DE21 4SZ.

ISBN 978-1-85983-776-4

Printed and bound by Cromwell Press Group, Trowbridge, Wiltshire.

INDEX OF WALKS

ACKNOWLEDGEMENTS

I wish to thank my friends Sue Broadrick and Pete Wallace for once again tirelessly checking the 30 walks in this book. Your diligence and commitment adds greatly to the accuracy of the instructions, something which I am sure is appreciated by its many users and certainly by me. I could not have done it without you.

I would also like to thank Steve Caron and the rest of the staff at Derby Books Publishing for their belief in my work, their past support and for their superb production, distribution and promotion of my Ghost Walks books.

It has been a pleasure to work with you all.

INTRODUCTION

This is a collection of 30 circular walks set in the delightful county of Leicestershire, the walks ranging from 1–10 miles in length. Each walk has at least one ghostly story attached to a part of it, some walks having several chilling tales, which, hopefully, will bring a shiver to even the warmest clad rambler! The stories include footpaths where you may encounter headless spirits or phantom cyclists, ghostly highwaymen, a profusion of nuns and grey or white ladies and a skeletal monk who roams Beacon Hill with his dog. You may hear the eerie sounds of ancient battles or observe Lady Jane Grey make her annual drive from Bradgate House to Newtown Linford church. One ghost you will not want to meet, Black Shug, is a fearsome beast the size of a wolf!

You should be warned that some of the ghosts are 'hands on', so you may be pushed or shoved in the back. One ghost has a predilection for women, so you may have your face stroked or your bottom patted. If you are a man, however, he may try to suffocate you.

The walks cover a wide range of Leicestershire scenery and take you to some of the less frequented parts of the county where you will be unlikely to see another walker. You will experience the superb variety of the countryside, enjoying the delights of rolling fields and the diversity of the National Forest. You can trek along windy ridges and craggy hilltops, explore wetlands, lakes and reservoirs, stroll along river valleys and climb to panoramic viewpoints.

On these quieter paths, you will find wildlife undisturbed by the tramp of many feet. Kestrels hover over pastures while the mewing cries of buzzards draw your eyes to their soaring flight. Jays and woodpeckers may be glimpsed in woodland, stately herons stand motionless in reed beds and, if you are lucky, an elusive kingfisher may imprint its brilliant hue on your day. Hares and foxes populate the fields and herds of red and fallow deer may be glimpsed in various areas. You will even see a herd of bison.

Leicestershire has a fascinating history and evidence of this abounds in its mediaeval villages, manor houses and stately homes. It is also reflected in its tales of witchcraft and sorcery and amusing legends, which are included in the walks.

As well as the ghostly tales, some of the walks include visits to famous halls and houses and the chance to see a number of fascinating churches, ranging from the beautiful St Luke's at Gaddesby to the tiny, exquisite Withcote Chapel, a hidden gem and surely one of Leicestershire's best-kept secrets.

Each walk has an introductory description, including the area covered, the type of terrain and highlighting its best attributes. Your attention is drawn to special features, such as a recommended time of year for doing the walk, for example late spring because the woods are full of bluebells and wild garlic.

The distance of each walk is given in miles and the walks are graded from A to C, i.e. from easy to energetic, with an explanation of the grades being provided at the front of the book.

Information is given regarding parking at the start of the walk, together with directions where thought necessary. A map grid reference is also stated.

Details of where refreshments may be obtained and WC facilities are identified where available, both at the start of walks and en route.

My friends and I have walked over 400 miles to put these walks together, compiling the routes and checking that the instructions are correct and as unambiguous as possible. The walk directions are very detailed and, hopefully, clear, and the text has been broken into numbered sections which relate to a sketch map. The sketch map also shows features such as farms, woods, roads and other points, which should assist you in navigation.

'Confirmers' – points that tell you that you are on the right path – are included throughout the instructions, and some, such as the name of a lane or farm, may be checked against an Ordnance Survey map if carried. If the instructions do not seem to match the terrain, stop and think for a moment. If necessary, retrace your steps to the last point where they fitted, rather than continuing and trying to make them fit.

A map is not essential for the walks, but information is given as to which Ordnance Survey map may be used. You may find one useful as an aid to navigation or in case you have to divert from the planned route due to, for example, flooding. It is also an easy way to get used to mapreading, by checking the walk instructions against a map and seeing how the information fits.

It has been my intention to produce a book which will be useful and interesting, intriguing and amusing and one which, while showing you the delights of the Leicestershire countryside, will also give you a taste of its rich folk history.

I hope that you will enjoy using it as much as I have enjoyed compiling it.

DEGREE OF DIFFICULTY

The walks are graded as follows, taking into account ascents, descents, terrain underfoot and length of walks. Grading may span two categories.

A. Easy: Gently undulating terrain. Taking into account the mileage, it should be well within the capabilities of regular walkers and fit occasional walkers.

B. Moderate: One or two longer or steeper ascents/descents but suitable for regular walkers who can manage the distance.

C. Energetic: Steeper ascents/descents, distance and rougher terrain make it a more demanding walk. Should be within the capabilities of reasonably experienced regular walkers.

EQUIPMENT:

Walking boots are recommended for all the walks. In view of the mileage, they will make even the walks graded A more enjoyable. In dry summer weather, lightweight boots would be suitable for A and B grades.

Suitable outerwear, including waterproof coats and trousers, hats and gloves, should be taken.

OTHER EQUIPMENT RECOMMENDED:

Food and drink: At least some emergency rations, e.g. chocolate for a quick energy boost. Also take plenty of water in summer to avoid dehydration and a hot drink in winter.

Compass

Whistle: For emergency use only.

Mobile phone: For summoning emergency assistance.

Torch (and spare batteries): In case you misjudge the time and night falls.

Survival bag or space blanket: Useful in case of accident to wrap casualty to keep them warm.

Rucksack: Leaves hands free.

First-aid kit: Containing plasters, blister kit and antiseptic cream.

Maps: Not essential as detailed instructions and a sketch map are provided. However, a map is useful as a back-up in case of confusion or in the event of diversion from the walk route due to adverse conditions such as flooding.

INFORMATION ON SKETCH MAPS:

FB   Footbridge

-------   Route

        Water

        Wood

        Sightings

OTHER TERMS USED IN TEXT:

Green lane – wide path, often grassy, between walls.

      Heading diagonally across field

     Bearing right, bearing left

     Bear left to 10 o'clock, bear right to 2 o'clock

     Turn through 180°

     Turn sharp left

WALK LOCATIONS

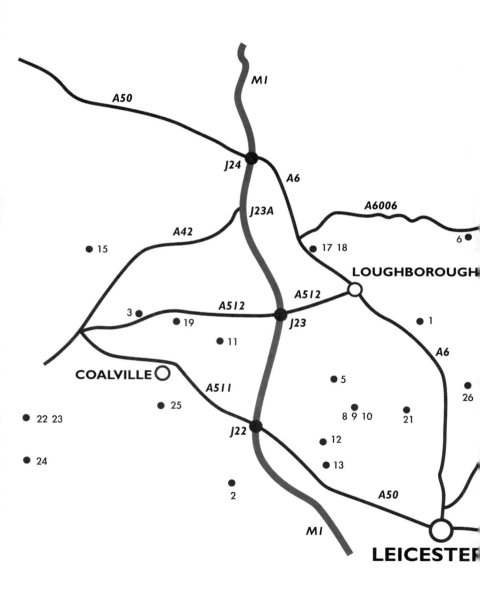

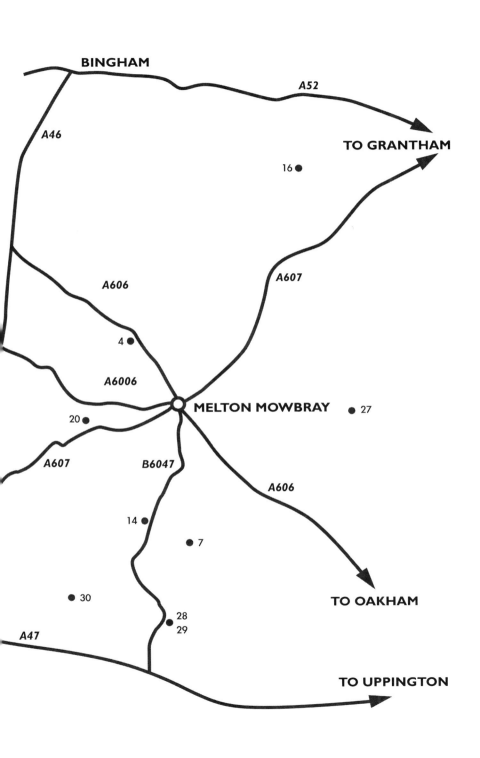

WALK 1
BARROW UPON SOAR
7½ miles

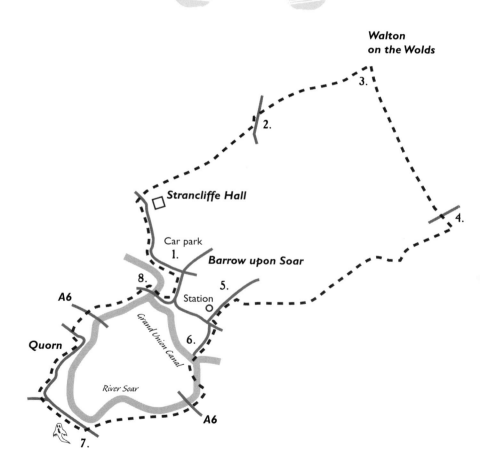

Walton on the Wolds

3.

2.

Strancliffe Hall

4.

Car park

1.

Barrow upon Soar

8.

5.

A6

Station

Grand Union Canal

6.

Quorn

River Soar

A6

7.

This walk shows the Wolds countryside at its best, with fine views of the Charnwood Hills. It returns through the water meadows of the River Soar as it curves away to Quorndon and back again.

NB: Do not attempt this walk if the river is in flood.

Distance: 7½ miles

Grade: A

Parking: Public car park adjacent to the Three Crowns pub at the junction of North Street, High Street and Cotes Road in Barrow upon Soar. There are two further car parks further along High Street. WCs in car park.

Map ref: SK 575175. Explorer 246 Loughborough, Melton Mowbray & Syston map.

Pub stop: Navigation pub (reached after 4½ miles).

ROUTE

1. Leave the car park by the entrance then turn right and immediately right again on to Cotes Road. Go ahead for ½ mile passing Humphrey Perkins High School and the impressive entrance of Strancliffe Hall. Continue to the end of the wall that fronts the gardens of the Hall then turn right on to a lane, a bridleway known as Strancliffe Lane. Where the rough surface of the lane ends, go ahead to walk between hedges, continuing on this pleasant path until you reach a road.

2. Turn left. After 100 yards turn right over a stile at a footpath sign. Cross a lane and a second stile then follow the direction of the footpath sign to walk diagonally across the field. Go over the stile on the far side then go straight ahead to walk with the hedge on your left. Go through a gate and continue in the same direction in the following field.

3. At the far side of the second field, do not go over stile. Instead, turn right to walk with the hedge on your left. The path bears slightly right to reach a gap in the far end hedge about 50 yards from the left-hand corner. Go down the green lane, walking between hedges. Continue to the bottom of the field where you cross Fishpool Brook, and then go through the gate and go ahead, now with the hedge on the right. Pass through another gate then walk between hedges to reach Melton Road.

4. Cross over and go straight ahead on to the bridleway opposite. On reaching a crossing of paths, go through the gate to the right then immediately bear right to reach a stile in the middle of the fence ahead (i.e. not on the path by the hedge). Cross the stile and continue in the same direction in the following field, to reach a stile in the right-hand corner. Go over the stile (not through the gateway) and over a second stile, then continue down the field with the hedge on your left. Go over another stile then turn diagonally right across the next field. In the following field, walk with the hedge on your right. Cross a track and a stile and continue with the hedge on your right for three more fields. Continue ahead in a small field at a crossing of paths. Go straight over the next two fields, following the yellow arrow signs. At the end of the second field, go ahead over a footbridge and on to the road. Turn left, then after 30 yards turn right to follow a footpath (alongside No. 61) leading you to the Melton Road.

5. Turn left. Go along the road for about 400 yards, passing the railway station to reach a T-junction. Turn left, then, after 30 yards, turn right on Ribble Drive. Continue ahead bearing right at the bottom to another

T-junction. Turn left. The Navigation pub is open all day to provide refreshment.

6. Cross the bridge over the Grand Union Canal. Go ahead with the weir to your left then turn left through a kissing gate and onto a path between fences. Go over the footbridge and continue. Go over a stile, then, where the path divides, take the right-hand one, heading for the main A6 road. Go under the road and follow the direction of the arrow sign in the field. Bear slightly right, joining the River Soar. Cross a footbridge then go straight ahead under the power lines leaving the river. Continue straight ahead for three more fields to reach the road.

Barrow upon Soar, where a headless ghost haunts the footpath.

7. Turn right. Keep straight ahead for 300 yards, then turn right on to School Lane. You continue on this road for another ½ mile, passing a footbridge over the river. Then, 300 yards after a sharp left-hand bend, turn right at a footpath sign (hidden in a tree) down Huntsman Close. Cross the footbridge over the A6 and keep ahead over the field to reach a road.

A headless phantom haunts this footpath which runs between Quorndon and Barrow upon Soar. Some ghosts appear headless because they were decapitated, either in an accident, in battle or were executed. In other cases the headless state can be because they lack the energy to fully materialise. Why this tortured soul should be without its head is not known.

8. Turn right and go over the bridge. Where the road forks, go left on High Street, signed 'Village Centre'. Continue up High Street to return to the car park.

WALK 2
THORNTON RESERVOIR
7½ miles

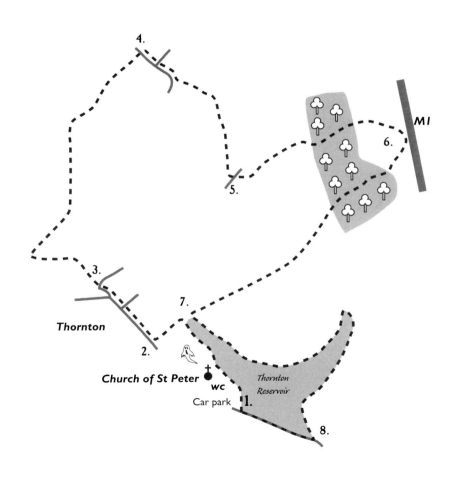

This is a pretty walk situated in an area between Coalville and Leicester. It is mostly on good paths and tracks, through fields and woods, and includes a circuit of the picturesque Thornton Reservoir.

Distance: 7½ miles

Grade: A

Parking: Car park on Reservoir Road, Thornton, adjacent to Thornton Reservoir. WCs at Visitors' Centre near start of walk. See instructions.

Map ref: SK 470075. Explorer 245 The National Forest or Explorer 233 Leicester & Hinckley maps.

Pub stop: None. Tea shop at Garden Centre to right of car park entrance.

ROUTE --

1. From the car park, facing the reservoir, take the path to the left to walk with the reservoir on your right. After 300 yards, you come to the Visitors' Centre and WCs. Continue in the same direction. After 100 yards you reach the path to the Church of St Peter.

There are reports of a ghost haunting the church and vicarage. The vicar was forced to perform an exorcism on his own home when his wife complained that it kept waking her in the night.

Continue until you see the end of the reservoir then turn left through a gate at a sign for Thornton Recreation Ground and Community Centre. Go up the hill, with the playground on your left and straight ahead to the road.

Church of St Peter, Thornton, where church and vicarage are haunted.

2. Turn right. Go past Markfield Lane on your right, then, at the next road junction, go straight ahead on Stanton Lane following the sign for Stanton.

3. Where the road bends to the right, leave it and go ahead through a gap stile at a public footpath sign. Where, after a few yards, the path forks, keep straight ahead. Go over a stile and follow the yellow arrow sign across the field. But on the far side, do not go ahead over the next stile. Instead, at a yellow post 20 yards before the stile, turn sharp right on a path up this same field. The marker arrow showing the direction is on the other side of the post. At the top of this field, pass under the power lines, go through an open gateway and turn left in the next field, to walk with a hedge on your left for two fields. In the third field, take the right-hand of two paths. On the far side go over the stile and turn left. Continue on a broad grassy path to a stile and sign for the Ivanhoe Way. Go down the next field to reach a road.

4. Turn right. Pass a road to the left, then where the road bends to the right, go ahead over a stile to walk with a hedge on your left. At the end of the field, on reaching stiles to the left and ahead, ignore these and instead turn right (not signed) to walk with a hedge on your left. Continue ahead, passing over a stile and a footbridge and by a lone picnic table until, eventually, you reach an iron gate. Go through it and over a footbridge and ahead to reach a road.

5. Turn left. Then, after 50 yards, turn right at a public footpath sign. Go over a stile at the sign for Lame Duck Farm.

Farmers in the past frequently named their holdings with wry humour denoting their opinion of the land from which they were trying to wrest a living. Place names such as Back Break Meadow or Sour Lands need no explanation of what they thought of them. It is not clear whether this farm has an ancient history or if this is a modern comment on a mistake. Or perhaps they simply have a lame duck!

Keep ahead on a track, then, after 100 yards, bear left over a stile then turn left in the field to walk with a hedge on your left. Keep straight ahead for two fields then continue in the same direction across a playing field. On the far side, go over the stile and turn right on a broad track. Then, after 30 yards, turn left at a yellow arrow sign. Follow this path as it meanders through woodland then continue ahead with a hedge on your left to eventually reach a stile by an iron gate. Go down a paved road towards the motorway.

6. At a second iron gate, turn right to walk with a fence on your left. Go through a gate at the end of the field then bear right in the two following fields. Follow the direction of the arrow sign on a broad grassy path through trees. At a crossing of paths, keep straight ahead down some steps and across a footbridge. Continue on a broad path between trees, emerging eventually into a large open field. Go straight ahead following an arrow sign, heading eventually for a stile by the side of an iron gate. Go over the stile and walk with a hedge on your right. Then go over a stile into the following field, walking now with a hedge on your left. At the end, where you see the reservoir to your left, go left through a gap and right and then straight ahead in the same direction as before, with a hedge on your right, to reach the end of the reservoir.

7. Go through the kissing gate and turn left on a broad path to walk with the reservoir on your right. Continue round the reservoir for 1½ miles, eventually reaching a road.

8. Turn right. After 500 yards you reach the entrance to the car park on your right.

WALK 3
COLEORTON
6¼ miles

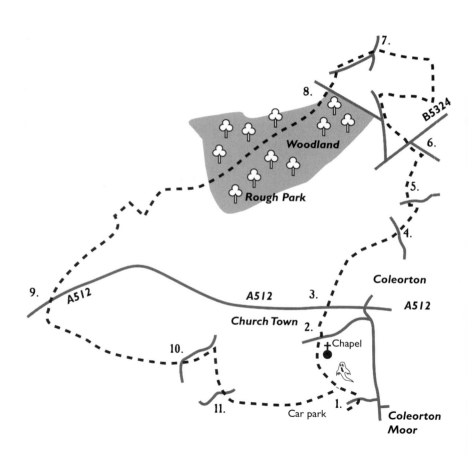

7.

8.

B5324

6.

Woodland

5.

Rough Park

4.

Coleorton

9.   A512   A512   3.   A512

Church Town   2.

+ Chapel

10.

1.

11.   Car park   Coleorton
                          Moor

This pleasant walk in an area to the east of Ashby de la Zouch is made even more enjoyable in spring by bluebells, rhododendrons and gorse. It is on good paths through fields, woodland and open countryside. NB: Some paths may be overgrown with nettles in summer.

Distance: 6¼ miles

Grade: A

Parking: Coleorton Wood. In the village of Coleorton Moor, turn off a road called The Moor onto Pitt Lane. Go down this narrow lane, continuing past the houses to reach a large parking area at the end. Note that this car park opens at 8.30am each day, but has different closing times through the year, e.g. 4pm in winter. Check the closing time on the notice board before commencing the walk.

Map ref: SK 400165. Explorer 245 The National Forest Map.

Pub stop: None on walk. The Angel in Coleorton Moor.

ROUTE -

1. Leave the car park by the entrance and go back up the road. Just past the houses turn left by Wisteria Cottage, through a gate (not signed). Go left down the field, through a kissing gate and follow the direction of the arrow sign down the next field with the hedge on your left. Cross a footbridge and a stile, then, at a division of paths, take the one to the right. Walking with the hedge on your right, continue to follow the boundary as it curves left and then turn right over a stile. In the field bear right, heading between the tiny St John's Chapel (formerly a mortuary chapel) and the buildings, crossing another stile and ahead to the road.

It was in this area of Corkscrew Lane that an old resident of Ashby was walking on a summer's evening in the 1950s. He was passing a copse when he heard the sounds of a battle coming from the other side of the trees. The sounds of horses neighing, voices shouting, the clash of swords on armour, the screams and loud groaning of men in pain continued for several minutes though the man could see nothing. Too afraid to satisfy his curiosity, he left the scene. On relating the story to friends, he found that many others

Corkscrew Lane. The ghostly sounds of a Civil War battle may still be heard.

had had the same experience at that spot. During the Civil War, there was a Royalist garrison at Ashby but the rest of the area supported the Parliamentary forces. The copse on Corkscrew Lane is the site of one of the many violent clashes between the two sides which has apparently echoed down the years.

2. Turn right, then, after 20 yards, turn left down some steps and over a stile at a footpath sign. Cross the field with the fence and wood to your right. Ignore the first stile to the right then go over the second. Bear left through the bushes then head for the lake in the distance. Pass a large gate to the left and continue for another 30 yards on a broad stony track. Then turn left on an overgrown path to a stile and yellow marker post hidden in the hedge leading onto the road.

3. Take care crossing the very busy A512 road, bearing right to a footpath on the far side. Following the direction of the arrow sign, go diagonally right to pick up a yellow arrow sign on a post about 100 yards ahead. From the post continue to follow the waymarker, crossing a footbridge and two more markers, to continue to the corner of the next field. Take the footpath to the left of the corner (note there is one to the right of it as well). Cross a second footbridge and a stile and follow the direction of the arrow sign in the field to reach another stile leading onto a road.

4. Turn left, then, after 20 yards, turn right at a footpath sign. Go straight ahead in the field, over a stile then bear left, following the direction of the arrow, to reach a stile just before the house. Cross the paved drive and go over some fencing at a yellow arrow sign. Follow the path with the hedge on your right, then, in the field, continue in the same direction to a footpath sign by the outbuildings of the house to your left. Cross a stile and go on to a lane.

5. Turn left, then, after 50 yards, turn right at a public footpath sign. Go through the gate and straight across the field (the sign is pointing incorrectly to the right). The next stile is in line with the telegraph pole and in the middle of the curved hedge ahead. Cross it and bear right following the arrow, joining a hedge on the right to reach a stile. Go over it and left on a path which follows the left-hand boundary, continuing on a rough track to reach a road.

6. Turn left. At the road junction (Rempstone Road) cross over to the public footpath sign and go on to a lane. Pass by an iron gate and a bungalow called The Gables and ahead to the road. Turn right on School Lane, passing the sign for Newbold. Then, as you reach the houses, turn right at a public footpath sign. Go over a stile into the field and walk with the hedge on your right. About 50 yards past the hedge in the middle of the field, which divides this field from the next, turn left up the field. At the top of the field do NOT go over the stile. Instead turn left (not signed) going back across the field to walk with the hedge on your right. At the corner continue ahead into a green lane, eventually reaching a road.

7. Turn left, then, after 30 yards, turn right, signposted 'Lount and Melbourne', on Ashby Road. Continue to the end of the houses and the 'national speed limit' sign, then turn left at a footpath sign. Go over the stile into the field and take the right-hand of two paths to walk with the fence on your right. On the far side go over the stile on to the road.

8. Cross over, bearing right to a footpath sign and an iron gate. Go ahead on a broad track. Keep straight ahead through woodland, ignoring paths to the right and left. Eventually you leave the woods. Continue ahead on a lane. Pass a track joining from the right. When you reach a T-junction, turn right, and then, at the next fork, go left. Go under a bridge beneath the A512 road.

9. When, after another 200 yards, the road ends, turn left through an open gateway and continue ahead. Go through another gateway and across the field with the hedge on your right. At the end of the field turn right, over a stile, past a pond. Cross a stile into the following field and ahead, still with the hedge on your right. Go over another stile and on to a lane.

10. Turn left. After 300 yards, turn right at a public footpath sign over a stile. Ignore the direction of the arrow sign. Instead turn immediately right through the top of the fence and then left, to go down the field with the fence on your left. Continue ahead where the fence ends, following an old line of trees and stumps, bearing left at the bottom to a gate. Go through the gate and straight ahead up the field with a fence to your left to reach a stile on to a lane.

11. Turn left, then, where the road bends left, go right at a public footpath sign. When you reach a stile with two waymarkers, follow the one indicating straight ahead (not right). Go down the field with the fence on your left to the stile and bridge at the bottom. Go straight up the next field, then, following the arrow signs, bear left in the one after. When you reach a yellow post where there is a choice of paths, follow the arrow pointing you down the right-hand one. At the bottom of the field, cross over a stile hidden in the hedge and a footbridge. Then go ahead up the field with a hedge on your right, retracing your steps from the start of the walk. Go through the kissing gate and bear right along the fence to reach the gate on to the road. Turn right back to the car park.

WALK 4
AB KETTLEBY
8 miles

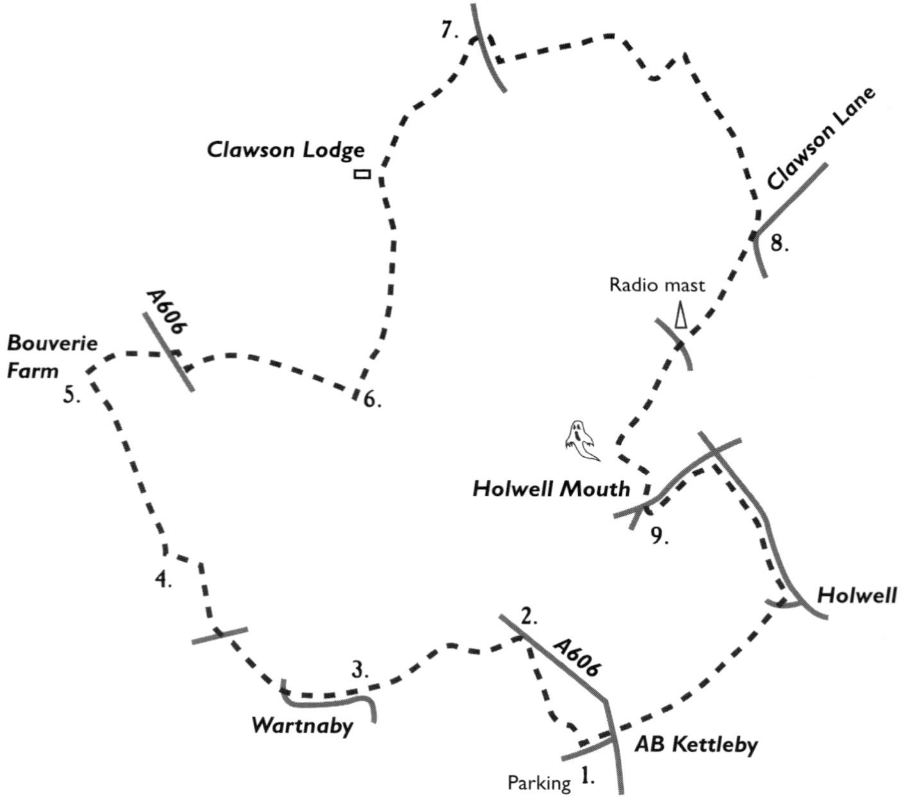

7.

Clawson Lodge

Clawson Lane

8.

Radio mast

Bouverie
Farm

A606

5.

6.

Holwell Mouth

9.

4.

Holwell

2.

A606

3.

AB Kettleby

Wartnaby

Parking   1.

This is an attractive undulating walk to the north of Ab Kettleby, with varied scenery and extensive views over the Vale of Belvoir. There is also some unusual wildlife to be seen, including the ghostly interest! Some paths and stiles may be overgrown in mid-summer.

Distance: 8 miles

Grade: B

Parking: On Wartnaby Road or roadside verge on Chapel Lane in Ab Kettleby.

Map ref: SK 724231. Explorer 246 Loughborough, Melton Mowbray & Syston map.

Pub stop: None.

ROUTE -

1. Take the footpath opposite No. 17 Wartnaby Road (Honeysuckle Cottage). Go between the houses, over a stile and straight ahead in the field. In the following field, bear left to a stile in the hedge. Turn right to walk with the hedge on your right for two fields. In the third field, go diagonally left to the corner where there are two metal gateways and the main road.

2. Do not go onto the road. Instead, turn left following the public bridleway sign, to walk with the hedge on your right. On reaching the corner, go through the metal gate and straight ahead across the field on the unploughed strip the farmer has left (official footpath goes right and then left through the crop), to reach double wooden gates and the road.

3. Turn right. At a junction, follow the road to the right, then, after 30 yards, turn left at the public footpath sign and follow its direction across the field. Go over a stile to reach a road. Cross over and turn left. After 50 yards, turn right at a footpath sign. Go through the iron gate and straight ahead in the field with the hedge on your right. Follow the path round to the left at the end of the field then, halfway along, turn right under the power lines at a yellow arrow sign.

4. Go down the slope, through the 7ft high kissing gate and to the left, to walk with the fence on your right. At the next fence, turn right down the hill, with the fence on your left.

A herd of bison may be seen in the fields to the right and left and, a little further on, two fields of deer.

Follow the arrow sign across the field and then go ahead down a lane, eventually reaching a junction at a sign for Bouverie Farm.

5. Turn right, passing a bungalow on the right. Go through an iron gate and continue ahead on a paved lane. After 100 yards, cross a stile on the right at a yellow footpath marker and go diagonally across the field to emerge on to the A606 main road. Turn right. After 50 yards, turn left at a footpath sign through an open gateway and straight ahead across the field. Go through another open gateway and turn right to continue with a hedge on your left, to reach a bridge and a stile in the far corner. Bear right and crawl under a strand of barbed wire after 5 yards. Go left along the hedge then bear right across the corner of the field, to reach a stile hidden in the hedge about 30 yards beyond it. Bear right to a gap in the hedge at the far end and a yellow post. Follow the direction of the arrow in the next field to reach a stile two-thirds of the way along the right-hand hedge.

6. This is a crossing of paths. Do not go over the stile. Instead, with your back to the stile, go straight across the field to a yellow post on the other side. Cross a bridge over the stream and straight ahead in the following field. Pass a gateway with yellow arrow signs to your right, continuing to the end and going through the small copse. Go straight across the next field, then bear right in the following field and ahead through some trees. On the far side of them, turn left through an open gateway, then turn right following the line of the hedge on your right-hand side. Cross a stile in the corner of the field, then go diagonally left to pass Clawson Lodge on your left-hand side. Continue to follow the yellow footpath marker signs for about ½ mile to emerge on to a road.

7. Turn right, then, after 200 yards, turn left at the bridleway sign. Go straight ahead across the next three fields. Continue between a fence and hedge to reach a lane. Turn right. At the end of the lane, go over a stile and ahead across the field, bearing left to a stile in the bottom left-hand corner. Go through a wooden gate and follow the blue arrow sign bearing left, continuing on a clear path through the woodland to reach another wooden gate into a field. Two thirds of the way up the field, when you reach a gate on the left, at a crossing of paths, turn right and go up the remainder of this large field with the hedge on your left. Go through a gateway and ahead, emerging eventually onto a road (Clawson Lane).

8. Turn right, then, after 50 yards where the road bends left, leave it to go ahead through a wooden gate at a yellow post. Go straight ahead across the field. Continue through a gate, onto a lane, reaching a road by a radio mast. Cross over, bearing left to a gate and a footpath sign. Go diagonally left across this large field. As you near the far side, look for a steep path up the bank to your left. This may be muddy and slippery. Alternatively, go to the end of the

Holwell Mouth, the haunt of a phantom hound known as Black Shug.

field and walk up by the fence. This will lead you to a stile in the top corner. Go through the metal gate into the woodland, on a meandering path, eventually reaching the road at Holwell Mouth.

This area used to be a pleasant bluebell wood, dropping down to a semi-circular dell with a spring in the middle of it. In the 18th century there were seats and an arch where people would come and picnic. However, they were careful not to stay after dark, as the woodland is the haunt of a phantom black hound. It is as big as a wolf and snarls at those who encounter it. Those unlucky enough to do so are also said to suffer a death in someone of their acquaintance. At one time the animal, known by some as Black Shug, roamed far and wide, but this century it has only been seen around Holwell Mouth. Thankfully, it confines its appearances to the hours between dusk and dawn, so as long as the sun has not set you should be safe!

9. Turn left. When you reach a road junction, turn right following the sign for Holwell. On entering the village, take the first right, Nursery Lane, following the sign for Ab Kettleby. Then, after 100 yards, turn left at a public bridleway sign and follow its direction across the field. Head diagonally left across the next field (two paths here) to a yellow marker in the top-left corner. Follow the direction of the arrow in the last field, joining a conifer hedge on your right, emerging onto the road in Ab Kettleby (A606). Go straight ahead down the Wartnaby Road to where you parked.

WALK 5
WOODHOUSE EAVES
8½ miles

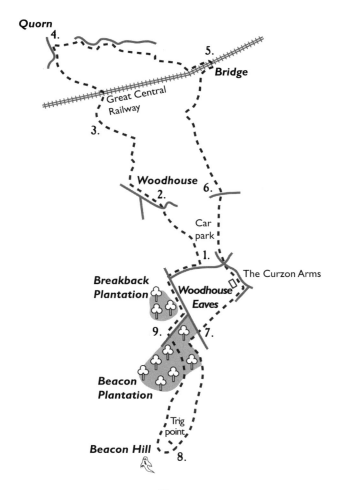

Quorn
4.

5.
Bridge

Great Central
Railway

3.

Woodhouse
2.   6.

Car
park
1.

The Curzon Arms

Breakback
Plantation   Woodhouse
Eaves

9.   7.

Beacon
Plantation

Trig
point

Beacon Hill
8.

This is an undulating walk with a wonderful variety of fields, woods, streams and villages full of character. It finishes with the panoramic viewpoint at Beacon Hill.

Distance: 8½ miles

Grade: B

Parking: Free car park on Main Street in Woodhouse Eaves with WCs.

Map ref: SK 530145. Explorer 246 Loughborough, Melton Mowbray & Syston map.

Pub stop: The Curzon Arms in Woodhouse Eaves, reached after about 5½ miles.

ROUTE --

1. Turn right out of the car park entrance then, after 20 yards, turn right at a public footpath sign. Go ahead on a clear path past a playground and playing fields on your right, continuing with a hedge on your left to a kissing gate. Cross the next field to a second gate and continue with a stream on your right to reach a lane and ahead to a road.

2. Turn left.

Note the beautifully thatched Pestilence Cottage on your left. A plaque a few yards further on gives you the story behind it.

Go up the road into the village of Woodhouse. At the road junction keep straight ahead, then, after 200 yards, turn right at a public bridleway sign on

Vicary Lane. Go ahead on the lane to a T-junction then turn left, signed 'The Wells House'. When you reach a yellow marker post, turn left, staying on the paved lane. Continue ahead where the lane becomes a rough track then, after 300 yards, turn right at a yellow arrow post.

3. Go between fields and then continue with the hedge on your right. Pass under the bridge beneath the railway then go ahead in a cutting or, if muddy, on a parallel path above to the left. When the path emerges into a field, cross it and go between hedges to reach a paved lane (Buddon Lane). At the end of the lane, go straight ahead on Chaveney Road. After 300 yards, just beyond No. 54, turn right at a public footpath sign.

4. Go straight ahead up a lane, then where it bends left leave it to go over a stile by a gate. At the next two gates, go over a stile and continue ahead for ½ mile on a winding path with a stream on your left, emerging eventually into a field. Continue with a hedge on your right then bear right to a stile and a yellow arrow. Go ahead on a narrow path between fence and hedge and then with an iron railing to your left. Cross a bridge then in the field beyond bear diagonally right.

On the far side, go ahead between fences adjacent to the railway on your right. Go over a stile and continue between fence and hedge, over a second stile to reach a lane.

5. Turn right, crossing the bridge over the railway, then immediately turn right down a path, walking with the railway again on your right. After 150 yards, when you reach a yellow arrow, turn left and go up the field. Go through the iron gate and ahead with a hedge on your right, then through another iron gate and follow the direction of the yellow marker across the field. When you reach the corner of the field, turn left to walk with the trees on your right. Continue in this field and the following one with the hedge on your right. Go through an iron gate, across a lane and through the gate on the other side. Keep the hedge on your right for one field. Cross another lane and continue in the same direction for two more fields, eventually reaching a road.

6. Cross over and go ahead in the field with the hedge on your left. Where the hedge goes left, leave it and continue straight ahead following a yellow marker to reach the corner of the field. Go through an iron gate onto a road. Go ahead, then, when you reach a crossroads, cross over and go up Maplewell Road. Pass the Post Office and you will find the Curzon Arms on the right-hand side. After another 100 yards, turn right up Mill Road. Continue ahead on a stony track and into woodland. At the end of the trees, go through an iron gate and cross the field with the fence on your right. Go through two more iron gates to reach a road.

7. Cross over and turn left on the horse and cycle track. Stay on this track for about a mile until you reach Beacon Hill. (WCs in car park.) From the notice board continue up hill to the beacon fire basket. Go ahead through an iron gate then turn right to a second gate and up to a trig point. To the west of the trig point there is a topograph showing what lies in all directions of this panoramic view.

At 803ft above sea level, Beacon Hill is the second highest point in Leicestershire and has spectacular views over the Trent and Soar Valleys. It was once a Bronze Age hill fort, but all that remains are the shallow ditches between the dry stone wall and the car park. Evidence of bronze having been melted and formed into tools has been found in recent times. The rocks around the summit date back about 700 million years to a time

Beacon Hill, haunted by a monk with a skeletal face and his ghostly dog.

when the area was under the sea. They were formed by volcanoes when the ash from different eruptions fell into the sea and settled on the sea bed. The colours, thicknesses and grain show the variety of volcanic activity over a period. The area around Beacon Hill is haunted by a monk. He roams the hillside in these parts with his phantom hound. He is said to have the grinning face of a skull.

8. From the topograph, retrace the path towards the last iron gate, but instead of passing through it, turn right and follow the track downhill, ignoring all tracks on either side to reach the Lower Car Park.

9. Turn right on the road.

This road is called Breakback Road, and there is Breakback Plantation to the left of you. This may be an ancient comment by a former tenant of the land, as farmers frequently named their plots with wry humour. Perhaps the land in this area was particularly hard to work or unproductive, as there is also a Hunger Hill to the south-east of Woodhouse Eaves.

When you reach a T-junction at the end of the road, turn left. Continue down to the signpost for Swithland and the Old Bull's Head on the corner and turn right up Main Street for 500 yards to return to the car park.

WALK 6
WYMESWOLD
9 miles

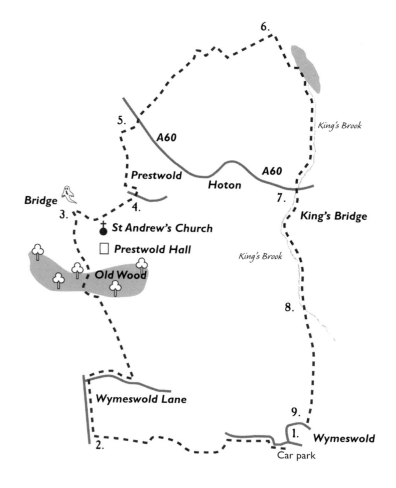

6.

King's Brook

5.

A60

Prestwold

Hoton

A60

Bridge

3.

4.

7.

King's Bridge

St Andrew's Church

Prestwold Hall

King's Brook

Old Wood

8.

Wymeswold Lane

9.

1.

Wymeswold

2.

Car park

This is a mainly flat walk on good paths with extensive views and a variety of scenery. It circles the village of Hoton, passing through the attractive Prestwold Park with its Hall and Church and returns along King's Brook.

Distance: 9 miles

Grade: A/B

Parking: Village Hall Car Park, Clay Street, off the Hoton Road, Wymeswold. There is an overspill car park at the back.

Map ref: SK 600234. Explorer 246 Loughborough, Melton Mowbray & Syston map.

Pub stop: None.

ROUTE -

1. Leave the car park by the entrance. Turn right on the road and right again on Hoton Road. Follow the road round to the right then, after 50 yards, turn left up Burton Lane. Turn left at the third footpath sign on the left and go ahead on a broad grassy path with a stream on your right. When you reach another footpath sign, turn right over the stile and go straight ahead across the field. Follow the direction of the arrow going straight ahead over the next field. Go through the copse and continue in the same direction in the field beyond. On the far side turn left, then after 50 yards, turn right to walk in the next field with the hedge on your right. Go ahead on a lane and continue to the road.

2. Turn right. Go along the road for ¼ mile then turn right on Wymeswold Lane. Turn left at the second footpath sign onto a broad path to walk with a dyke on your right-hand side. Continue to the wood, ignoring a path to the right, and follow the field boundary round to the left. Go through the open gateways then turn right, walking with the wood on your right. Go ahead into the wood.

After 20 yards note the parish boundary stone on the right. This footpath follows the route of the old highway, which ran from Six Hills on the A46 Fosse Way via Burton and Prestwold to the river crossing at Cotes.

Where the path divides, bear right. On the far side of the wood, continue ahead on a path with the dyke and Prestwold Hall to your right until you reach an old brick bridge.

3. Turn right over the bridge and head for St Andrew's Church. Go into the churchyard. This is a pleasant place for a break and the site of two stories connected with the church and surrounding area.

Early in the 16th century, in the midst of a three-month drought, Gertrude Lacey awoke in the middle of the night after a particularly vivid dream. She told her sister Grace that she had dreamt that she had found a new spring. She could even remember the exact location of it, Langdale field, behind Gorse Farm, which lay between the villages of Hoton and Wymeswold. She was carrying a staff from the Holy Land and when she drove it into the ground, water bubbled out. Grace was disbelieving at first but when the dream repeated a second and a third time, the sisters decided to tell the rest of the people in the village of Hoton, where they lived.

The villagers were keen to investigate and fortunately someone was able to produce a staff that a pilgrim had brought back from Canaan.

When they reached the field, Gertrude pushed the staff into the ground and clear water flowed out. The spring has never run dry since.

A stone structure was built around Two Sisters' Well, but this was dismantled in the early 1940s and the spring now flows into a culvert.

There is an effigy in St Andrew's Church of two ladies, which is said to date from about 1520, and local legend says that they are Gertrude and Grace Lacey and formerly there was a staff standing between them.

St Andrew's Church, the resting place of the Lacey sisters and the tragic Bellamont sisters.

Also, buried here are the Bellamont sisters, who were responsible for the building of Swarkestone Bridge. This impressive structure, which crosses the River Trent and low-lying marshland, is almost a mile in length and is the longest stone bridge in England. It was built in the early 13th century as the result of a tragic love story.

When the two sisters of the Bellamont family became betrothed, they decided to celebrate. On the day of the party, their fiancés had to attend a meeting with the barons on the far side of the River Trent, and while they were there a storm caused the river to become swollen. Anxious to return to the celebrations and their beautiful women, the men attempted to ford the river on horseback, but were swept away by the torrent and drowned.

The Bellamont girls built the bridge over the Trent to prevent anyone else suffering the same tragedy. They never married, and having spent so much money on the bridge, died in poverty and were buried together in this churchyard in one grave.

Unhappily, legend has it that they do not lie peacefully in their last resting place, as their ghosts are said to haunt the bridge on stormy nights, searching the raging river for their lost loves.

With the church to your right, leave the churchyard by the gate ahead and go onto the gravelled lane. Go straight ahead, crossing the driveway, then go through an iron gate and continue on a woodland path to reach a road.

4. Cross over the road, bearing left to a footpath on the far side. Go into the field and turn left, walking with a hedge on your left. As you approach the next field, turn right just before it (not signed) and walk with the trees on your left. When you emerge into the following field, turn right on a broad track to reach a road (A60).

5. Turn left, then after 30 yards turn right at the public footpath sign. Go ahead for ¾ mile on a lane, continuing through the farm and the field beyond. Turn right on a track for 1½ fields to reach a footpath sign after 200 yards. Turn left and go down to the bottom of the field with the hedge on your left.

6. Turn right. Go ahead with the brook on your left-hand side as the path winds left. Bear left at a footpath sign. Continue walking with King's Brook on your left-hand side for about a mile, ignoring all paths to left and right until you reach a road (A60) at King's Bridge.

7. Turn left over the bridge and immediately right onto the footpath on the far side, by climbing over the crash barrier at the side of the Leicestershire County sign. Go ahead on a path now with King's Brook on your right.

8. After about ¾ mile, turn right at a footpath sign, crossing the brook. Go through the gate and diagonally left across the field. Continue in the same direction for two more fields, then, in the third field, go ahead adjacent to the hedge on your right then with a wood to your left. Go straight on for two more fields then through the houses on Farriers Close to reach the road at Old Well Cottage.

9. Turn right, then, just past the allotments, turn left on a paved footpath. At the far end turn left and left again back into the car park.

WALK 7
BURROUGH HILL
8½ miles

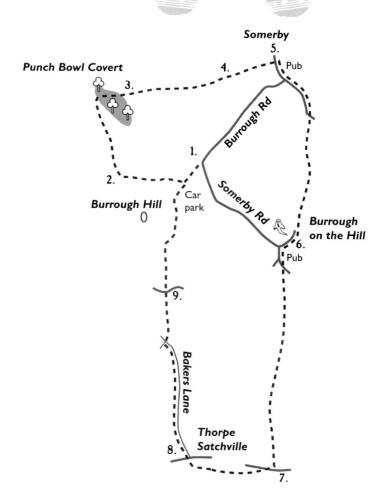

Somerby

5.

Pub

Punch Bowl Covert

3.

4.

Burrough Rd

1.

2.

Car park

Somerby Rd

Burrough Hill

0

Burrough on the Hill

6.

Pub

9.

Bakers Lane

Thorpe Satchville

8.

7.

This is a lovely walk from Burrough Hill Country Park, taking in the villages of Somerby and Thorpe Satchville. It has wonderful open views and is mostly on good paths, although some may be overgrown in summer.

Distance: 8½ miles

Grade: B

Parking: Car park at Burrough Hill Country Park (small charge).

Map ref: SK 767115. Explorer 246 Loughborough, Melton Mowbray & Syston map.

Pub stop: The Stilton Cheese Inn, Somerby and the Stag and Hounds, Burrough on the Hill.

ROUTE ---

1. Leave the car park by the lane opposite the entrance, marked 'Burrough Hill and Dolby Hills Path'. Go through the wooden gate and ahead on a broad track. After 300 yards, opposite a farm, turn right at a footpath sign and follow the direction of the arrow across two fields on the Jubilee Way to the top right-hand corner of the second. Go through the small gate, cross the field and go through a five-bar gate before heading down into a hollow to reach a yellow marker post.

2. Turn right and go through the gate into the trees (signed Dolby Hills Path). On the far side of the wood, go through a gate and straight ahead on a broad path. As you re-enter woodland, turn right past the sign for the Dolby Hills Path and go through the gate. Go ahead with the hedge on your right and up the hill to the stile at the top.

3. Turn right on a broad path (the right of way goes diagonally down the field, but the farmer has left a broad track around the edge). Stay adjacent to the field boundary on your right as it turns left, down the hill. At the end of this field, turn left for 50 yards to a yellow marker and stile and follow the direction of the arrow down the next field.

NB: When crops are grown, it is better to stay adjacent to the hedge on the right on the broad path that the farmer has left rather than trying to follow the actual footpath.

Climb the hill, staying on the track as it winds left and right. Keep straight ahead at a yellow marker into the next field. Where the field boundary swings to the right (with an old barn diagonally to your right), leave the track and go straight ahead to a stile in the hedge.

4. Go down the slope, then bear left and right through the trees to a yellow marker and bridge. This path is hidden in the trees and takes you down to a plank bridge over the stream, through a boggy area and then up the hill to a stile. Go ahead in the field with the hedge on your left. At the end, go right to the stile then straight ahead to a second stile, then across four fields and on a narrow path to reach the road in Somerby.

5. Turn right. Your pub stop, the Stilton Cheese Inn, is on your left. Continue along the main road to the corner where the Burrough Road goes right. Bear left, by the sign for Somerby Riding School, and go ahead on the tree-lined lane, ignoring the bridleway to the left. Where the road bends to the left, at a public footpath sign, bear right through the iron gate and into the field with the hedge on your left. Go through a small iron gate and ahead on a broad grassy path. As you approach the gorse bushes near the end of the field, turn right down the hill to a yellow marker post. Bear right down to another arrow post in the hedge. Go over two stiles and then across the field to a stile in the centre of the end hedge. Walk parallel to the hedge on your right. When you come to a stile go over it onto a paved lane and turn left.

6. At a T-junction turn right. Then at the road junction bear left, signposted 'Twyford', going onto Main Street. Your second pub is on your left, the Stag and Hounds. Follow the road as it bends to the left then, just past the 50mph limit sign, turn right at a bridleway sign to Twyford Lodge.

Burrough on the Hill, where a ghostly child haunts the roadside.

In the early 1990s, as dusk was falling on a winter's evening, an ambulance was travelling on this road having just left Burrough on the Hill. Out of nowhere it seemed a small child appeared dressed only in a nightgown or thin petticoat. The driver and his assistant both saw her and the vehicle pulled over, concerned that so young a child should be out alone at this time of night and in such cold weather. They left the ambulance and searched the area but found no sign of her, although there was not anywhere that she could have gone in so short a time.

Follow the direction of the post on a broad path across three large fields. Then, at a junction of paths, keep straight ahead in a fourth field. In the following two fields continue in the same direction with a hedge on your right. Then follow the direction of the marker post across two more fields to reach a road.

7. Turn right, then after 50 yards turn left at a footpath sign. Go over the stile and follow the direction of the arrow, bearing right up the field, keeping the barn on the horizon to your left. Go over the stile and ahead, crossing over a paved lane to a stile in the right-hand corner. Keep straight ahead in the next two fields, then through the churchyard to reach a road. Turn right to reach a main road.

8. Cross over, bearing left onto Bakers Lane.

Note the Millennium Milestone with the distances to Jerusalem and the North and South Poles.

At the next road keep straight ahead on Bakers Lane. Stay on this lane for ¾ mile, then where the road swings left, turn right, marked 'Leicestershire

Round Burrough Hill 1m', ignoring the green lane ahead. Go down the field, passing through a large gap in the hedge, continuing to the bottom left-hand corner and a marker post. Go ahead on a broad track to reach a road.

9. Cross over onto a path signposted 'Burrough Hill ½ mile' and go up the field with a hedge on your left. At the top of the field, follow the hedge round to the right and go through two gates. Bear right on a broad grassy path below Burrough Hill, which is to your left. Bear right through a five-bar gate and go down the lane to reach the car park.

WALK 8
BRADGATE PARK
4½ miles

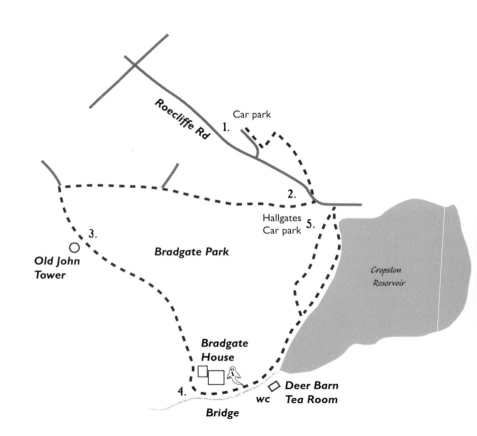

Roecliffe Rd

Car park

1.

2.

Hallgates Car park

5.

3.

Old John Tower

Bradgate Park

Cropston Reservoir

Bradgate House

4.

Bridge

WC

Deer Barn Tea Room

Bradgate Park is an oasis of tranquillity, its myriad paths absorbing the million visitors it receives each year. If you are really averse to crowds, visit midweek and wander its crags and tracks. This walk may be joined to Walk 9 Cropston for a longer route.

Distance: 4½ miles

Grade: A

Parking: Swithland Wood. Access from Roecliffe Road, near Hallgates entrance to Bradgate Park. Honesty box. WCs are available in Hallgates Car Park, Bradgate Park, ½ mile into the walk.

Map ref: SK 538118. Explorer 246 Loughborough, Melton Mowbray & Syston map.

Pub stop: No pub but Deer Barn Tea Room is reached after three miles. It sells a variety of light snacks and drinks. Opening times: April to October daily except Mondays. Weekdays 11am to 5pm, weekends 10.30am to 5pm. November to March Thursday and Friday 11am to 4pm, Saturday and Sunday 10.30am to 4pm.

ROUTE

1. Return to the short access road, but turn left by the side of the wooden gate and go down the broad track for 200 yards. At a yellow marker post, go right down some steps and ahead on the path alongside a stream. After 50 yards turn right over a stile and go diagonally left in the field, heading for the end of a line of trees, then bear right to the houses. Go over the stile and left on the road. After 30 yards, opposite Horseshoe Cottage Farm, turn right at a public footpath sign onto a lane.

If WCs are required, after 20 yards turn left on a grassy path which leads you to a gate into Hallgates car park.

Go ahead on the stony lane, which becomes a narrow path between a wall on the left and woodland on the right. Stay on this path for just over ½ mile, then 150 yards after you leave the trees, where a footpath comes in from the right, turn left through a kissing gate into Bradgate Park.

2. Turn right. Walk with the wall/hedge on your right until you reach the access road from the next car park coming in from your right. Turn left here up to Old John Tower.

Having reached the tower, enjoy the panoramic view as depicted by the topograph. This folly is said to have come about as the result of a tragic accident. In 1786, at the celebration for the fifth Earl's son coming of age, John, an old miller who liked his ale, was set the task of building and tending a massive bonfire here. A huge pole from the centre of the fire fell and killed him. From a certain angle the folly can be seen to look like an ale tankard. In later times hound and horse racing took place and this spot was used as a grandstand.

3. To leave the tower, with your back to the green memorial plaque to Charles Bennion, go straight ahead down a broad grassy path. After 300 yards take the first path to the right by two outcrops of rock. When you meet another path, bear right, ignoring the path that crosses it, then where the path divides take the right-hand fork. Stay on this path, crossing two tracks, eventually skirting a wood on your right. Go through the open gateway ahead and down to the ruins of Bradgate House.

Bradgate's most famous ghost is that of Lady Jane Grey, who on New Year's Eve is said to leave the old ruins of her childhood home in a coach pulled by four black horses. Most visitors congregate on the main paved path, but the original drive route was from the back of the house so your present approach would be a better viewpoint.

The coach with its lonely occupant drives to Newtown Linford church and disappears, reappearing nine days later and returning.

Lady Jane is not the only ghostly resident of the park. Some late visitors sitting near the bridge over the River Lyn heard the voices of a crowd of people approaching, but they waited in vain for them to appear. The sound passed by them and faded.

One evening in April 1995 three sharp bangs like a drum being struck were heard to come from the ruins. The visitors felt a dreadful change in the atmosphere. It felt as though something were about to happen and they saw the birds and deer scatter from the area. Then there were three more bangs and the oppressive feeling lifted and the animals returned.

One weekday spring morning a woman taking her grandchildren for a stroll, accompanied by her Scottish terrier, walked up to the ruins to check the opening time, leaving the children by the path below. As she neared the ruins, her dog started barking hysterically and she saw a man approaching. He wore an eye-patch on his weather-beaten features and his hair was tied back in a ponytail. He was dressed in a brown coat and riding boots and she presumed he was one of the rangers. She was about to ask him a question when he strode past her and straight through the wall, at which point she realised he was a ghost.

Opening times of the ruins: April to October, Wednesday, Thursday, Saturday, 2pm to 5pm. Sunday 10am to 12.30 and 2pm to 5pm.

Go past the ruins bearing left on a grassy path to reach the main paved track opposite a stone bridge.

It is at this point that the walk may be joined to Walk 9 Cropston at Section 3 by going over the stone bridge and following the instructions from there.

Bradgate House, the site of many strange happenings.

4. Turn left on the paved lane. After 600 yards you will reach Deer Barn Tea Room. There are accessible WCs here without using the Tea Room.

Continue on the paved lane for 300 yards until you meet a copse of trees on the left-hand side opposite a bench. You may at this point stay on the paved lane back to Hallgates car park.

Alternatively, for a more interesting and scenic route, turn left on a broad grassy path, with the trees on your right. Just before an open gateway, turn right up a narrower path between the bracken, up to the trees on the skyline and continue in the same direction with the wall and trees on your left. This stony path winds around the trees with a good view of Cropston Reservoir to the right. It then drops down to Hallgates car park.

5. Go through the kissing gate into the car park and leave by the entrance opposite. Turn left on the road, then just past Horseshoe Cottage Farm, go over the stile marked Swithland Wood. Follow its direction across the field, retracing your route from the beginning of the walk, to reach a stile in the right-hand fencing, 50 yards from the corner. Turn left and after 50 yards go up the steps and left on the track back to the car park.

WALK 9
CROPSTON
4¾ miles

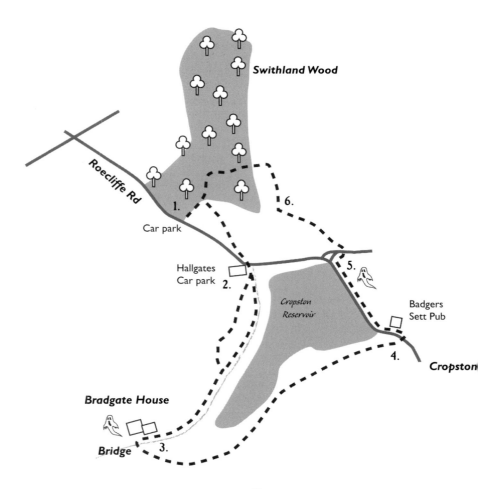

Swithland Wood

Roecliffe Rd

1.
Car park

6.

Hallgates
Car park 2.

Cropston
Reservoir

5.

Badgers
Sett Pub

4.

Cropston

Bradgate House

Bridge 3.

This is a pleasant walk including part of Bradgate Park then taking you away from the crowds on a tranquil circuit of Cropston Reservoir. It has excellent views on good paths, although some may be rather overgrown in summer.

This walk may be joined to Walk 10 Swithland for a longer route.

Distance: 4¾ miles

Grade: A

Parking: Swithland Wood. Access from Roecliffe Road, near Hallgates entrance to Bradgate Park. Honesty box.
WCs are available in Hallgates Car Park, Bradgate Park, ½ mile into the walk.

Map ref: SK 538118. Explorer 246 Loughborough, Melton Mowbray & Syston map.

Pub stop: Badgers Sett, Cropston. Also refreshments available at Deer Barn Tea Rooms, reached after 1¼ miles. This sells a variety of light snacks and drinks. Opening times: April to October, daily except Mondays. Weekdays 11am to 5pm, weekends 10.30am to 5pm. November to March, Thursday and Friday 11am to 4pm, Saturday and Sunday 10.30am to 4pm.

ROUTE -

1. Return to the short access road but turn left by the side of the wooden gate and go down the broad track for 100 yards. At a yellow marker post, go right down some steps and ahead on the path. After 50 yards turn right over a stile and go diagonally left in the field, heading for the end of a line of trees, then bear right to the houses. Go over the stile and left on the road. Go past

Horseshoe Cottage farm and turn right into Hallgates car park. WCs are to the right.

2. Cross the car park and go through the kissing gate opposite the entrance. Here you have a choice of routes. You may remain on the paved lane ahead of you for 1¼ miles until you reach the ruins of Bradgate House on your right and a stone bridge to your left.

Alternatively, for a more interesting and scenic route, bear right just past the 'Welcome to Bradgate' sign and go up the hill, keeping the two picnic tables to your right, heading for the copse of trees on the skyline.

Stay on this stony path as it winds around the trees and wall on your right. When the path starts to swing away from the trees on the far side, leave it and go down between the bracken and then left on a wider track where there is an open gateway to your right. Pass a copse of trees on your left. When you reach the paved lane, turn right, passing Deer Barn Tea Rooms (WCs on main path) to reach the ruins of Bradgate House after 600 yards.

(See Walk 8 for details of ghost stories around the ruins)

3. Turn left over the stone bridge opposite the ruins, going onto the stony track. Where the track swings right, where there is a seat ahead, turn left onto the first of two grassy paths going across the meadow. On the far side, go through the kissing gate and across the middle of the field, heading for the right-hand corner. Go on to a stony path, then, after 50 yards, turn right over a stile in the fence and left on the path between fences. Cross another stile and straight ahead in the field. In the following field, walk around two sides of it with the hedge on your left. Pass through a small wooden gate then walk in the next field with the hedge on your right. At the end of the second field go onto a stony lane then ahead on a road (Causeway Lane) to reach the main road.

4. Turn left on Reservoir Road. Your pub stop, the Badgers Sett, is on the right-hand side. Cross the end of the reservoir.

Cropston Reservoir, where a ghostly carriage surprised a milkman.

Twelve farms were flooded when Cropston Reservoir was created in 1869. It covers 200 acres and was stocked with fish. In July 1969, a relief milkman in an electric milk float was driving along this road. Ahead of him he saw a carriage pulled by two horses cross the road from right to left and disappear. When he arrived at the point where the carriage had vanished he realised that all that was to the left were the waters of the reservoir. The wall was unbroken and there was nowhere else for it to have gone.

5. On the far side of the reservoir, turn right on Lodge Lane, signposted 'Swithland 1½'. At Bradgate Road cross over and turn right. Then, after 70 yards, turn left at a yellow arrow over a stile. Go ahead on a path between a hedge and a wood. When you emerge into a field, remain adjacent to the hedge on your right. Pass a high seat and a small lake, where a stately heron may be glimpsed among the reeds and bulrushes. Continue on a path, which gets rather overgrown in summer, to reach a stile. Go ahead with a fence on your right. Go over a second stile, passing between hedge and sheds and continuing on a clear path to a stile and yellow marker post.

6. Turn right through the metal gate and ahead on a wide path. At the next marker post, turn left, then enter Swithland Wood going ahead on a broad path. When you reach a main track crossing your own where there is fencing opposite, turn left.

If you wish to join Walk 10, the Swithland walk, to this one, turn right here and join the instructions from section 2.

Continue on this broad path until you reach the access road to the car park. Turn right back to the parking area.

WALK 10
SWITHLAND
3 miles

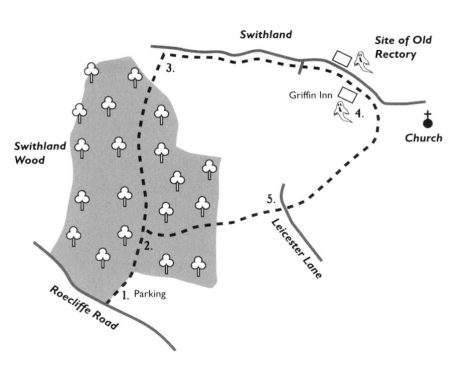

Swithland

Site of Old
Rectory

3.

Griffin Inn

4.

Church

Swithland
Wood

Leicester Lane

5.

2.

1. Parking

Roecliffe Road

This is a lovely walk through the broadleaf beauty of Swithland Wood, which is full of bluebells in spring. It visits the pretty village of Swithland with its interesting properties and ghostly tales before returning across the fields on good paths.

This walk may be joined to Walk 9 Cropston for a longer route.

Distance: 3 miles

Grade: A

Parking: Swithland Wood. Access from Roecliffe Road, near Hallgates entrance to Bradgate Park. Honesty box.

Map ref: SK 538118. Explorer 246 Loughborough, Melton Mowbray & Syston map.

Pub stop: Griffin Inn, Swithland.

ROUTE -

1. Return to the short access road, but turn left by the side of the wooden gate and go down the broad track for 200 yards, crossing a stream and a footpath to the right. Continue for another 300 yards, passing a mound followed by some wooden fencing on the left and another path to the right.

2. Keep straight ahead but look for a plaque on the right informing you that Swithland Wood was secured as a National Heritage Site by the Rotary Club of Leicester in 1931. Just beyond this, where the paths divide, take the right-hand one downhill, continuing through this pleasant woodland for another ¼ mile. Cross a more open area then keep straight ahead, ignoring two paths to the left. Go over a stile and walk between fields to reach a road.

3. Turn right. Walk through the attractive village of Swithland, with its extensive, luxurious properties and further on older period cottages and ones with thatched roofs.

As you approach the other end of the village, the Griffin Inn is ahead of you. On the left, just before the school, is the site of the Old Rectory where the tragic story of the Lady in Grey has its origins.

Back in 1820 the family occupying the Old Rectory went away for a holiday in Yorkshire leaving Parker, their butler, at the house alone. At the end of the holiday, the rector decided to send his 20-year-old daughter home early to prepare for their return. When she arrived she found Parker's appearance alarming. He looked as though he had been drinking heavily and was still drunk.

She decided that it was prudent to stay out of his way and retired to her bedchamber, resolving to stay awake all night if necessary. But the long hours she had spent on the coach from Yorkshire took their toll and she fell asleep still wearing her grey brocade travelling dress.

The crash of her bedroom door in the middle of the night awoke her and before she could even scream, the drunken butler was upon her.

Having passed out, Parker came to some hours later and found a horrendous sight. He had murdered the daughter and she was hanging from one of the beams of the four-poster bed. Realising that he would be executed for the crime, he fetched a knife and hacked at his throat until he choked on his own blood and died. The family returned to the horrific scene of a murder and suicide.

For many years, villagers heard terrifying screams emanating from the rectory and saw the ghost of the butler staggering about, hacking at his throat. These hauntings ceased after World War One when the rectory was pulled down. Then reports came of the ghost of a lady dressed in grey in the

St Leonard's Swithland, still haunted by the tragic Lady in Grey.

churchyard of St Leonard's, appearing at weddings, christenings and funerals and even at a garden party. More recently, the phantom was seen by one of the male bellringers at evening practice as she drifted across the churchyard. So it would seem that the spirit of this tragic young girl is still not at rest after all these years.

The Griffin Inn also has its ghostly occupants. The restaurant at the pub was once used as a mortuary and a darkish figure is said to have been seen walking straight through what is now the fireplace. An ancient annexe is situated behind the restaurant and is reached by a small staircase. It was on these stairs that a ghostly hand gave a member of staff a firm shove in the back.

If you wish to visit the church of St Leonard's, it is 100 yards beyond your turn on to the footpath.

4. As you reach the end of the houses on the right, turn right at the footpath sign. Go down a narrow path and through two iron gates. In the field, go straight across to a yellow marker post. Continue on a clear path between fields to reach a road.

5. Cross over and turn right. Then, after 30 yards, go left at a public bridleway sign. Stay on this path, re-entering Swithland Wood after ¼ mile. When you reach a path crossing your own, where there is wooden fencing opposite, turn left. Continue on this broad path until you reach the access road to the car park. Turn right back to the parking area.

WALK 11
MOUNT ST BERNARD
ABBEY
7 miles

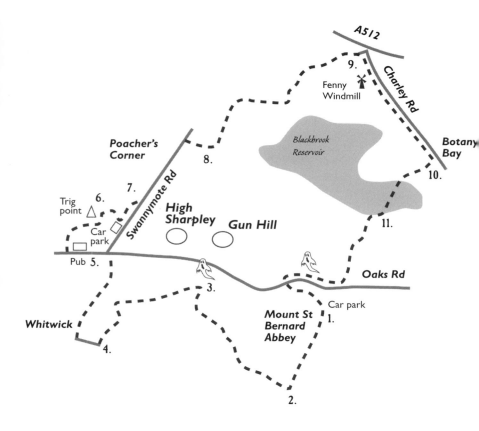

This is an interesting undulating walk, using minor roads, tracks and paths. It has a wonderful variety of scenery going through woods and fields and across a reservoir, with extensive views at several points.

Distance: 7 miles

Grade: A/B

Parking: Car park, Mount St Bernard Abbey, Oaks Road, Whitwick. WCs in car park.

Map ref: SK 459162. Explorer 245 The National Forest map.

Pub stop: Man Within Compass, Whitwick.

ROUTE --

1. Leave the car park at the footpath sign which is to the left when facing the WCs and go ahead on the lane for ¼ mile. At a T-junction, with a gate to the left, bear right and then left to reach the end of the lane.

2. Turn right to walk with a wall on your right. There are good views of the Abbey and countryside beyond at this point. Continue into woodland then go right along the top of a field. Re-enter the wood and go straight on with a wall on your right. Bear right onto a broad track, then, leaving the track, bear left at a yellow arrow sign on a narrower path. Climb up at the side of Whitlock Quarry, eventually bearing right downhill to walk with a wall on your right. Pass a footpath on the right which heads towards the Abbey. Pause at a second footpath sign where your path turns left.

If you face the footpath sign, the tree-clad hill beyond it is **Gun Hill**, with **High Sharpley** to the left, where the tragic ghost of **Lady Aslin** wanders.

In the 13th century, at the time of King John, Goisfried Aslin was the disreputable Lord of Whitwick Castle. He spent his time in drunken orgies and every kind of sexual depravity. Then one day he met and fell in love with Gertrude Lyne, a young country girl. For a time he seemed a reformed character, but then he returned to his old ways.

After forcing his wife to watch a despicable orgy, he informed her that in future she would have to join in. He ignored her pleas and tears, and, rather than face this, Lady Aslin left the castle that night and headed for High Sharpley. She was later found drowned in Blackbrook Pool. Her lonely ghost is said to have haunted the hills of High Sharpley and Gun Hill since that time.

3. Turn left then keep straight ahead. When you emerge into a field, follow the direction of the arrow bearing slightly left, heading for the houses to reach a road.

4. Turn right. Just past No. 77 turn right at a sign for the Ivanhoe Way. Go up the path, cross a road and continue in the same direction. Go into a field and walk with the hedge on your right. Stay on this path for ½ mile, then head down to a road to be seen ahead. Go over a stile onto a short lane and turn left to the road.

5. Turn left along Loughborough Road. After 300 yards you reach the strangely named pub, 'Man Within Compass'. Just beyond the pub, turn right at a public footpath sign adjacent to No. 127. Follow the footpath sign over the grassy area and through the gap in the wall into the wood. Turn right on the path just inside and stay on it to reach a yellow arrow. Go ahead uphill with a large rocky outcrop to your right. At the top of the short rise, turn right on a path running above the outcrop with it still on your right. The path bends left, passing another rocky outcrop on the right. Keep straight ahead for another 100 yards. When you come to a fork in the path, go left to pass between a large rock on the left and a small low one on the right. Continue ahead past high ground to be glimpsed through the trees to your left. Then, where the path divides, go left on a path curving to the left uphill, to cross an open area and reach a trig point and a wonderful view.

Mount St Bernard Abbey, where Brother Holland's ghost was seen.

6. With your back to the path you have just come up and facing the trig point, turn right and go down a narrow but clear path, dropping steeply down to reach another path crossing your own. Turn right. After 200 yards, when you see a road ahead, take a narrow path to the left. This path is 50 yards before a small car park and it may be easier to retrace your steps from the car park to ensure you have the right one. The path eventually reaches a broad path crossing your own where you bear right to a yellow marker post. Just beyond this post, where the path divides, go left, with a wall on your left. Continue on this path until you emerge onto the road (Swannymote Road).

7. Turn left. Stay on this road for ½ mile then, at a crossroads called Poacher's Corner, turn right.

8. After ¼ mile turn left at the footpath sign to Sandhole Lane. Go straight ahead in the field with a hedge on your left. Turn right along the top side. Then, at the corner of this field, bear left following the arrow sign. Drop down the next field, then, at the lowest point, turn right and through a wooden gate. Go ahead down a narrow track to reach a lane. Turn left. The lane winds right and left then climbs. At the top of the rise, go right through a gap stile at a yellow marker. Bear left, following the direction of the arrow up the field to reach a stile leading onto a lane.

9. Turn right and right again at the main road.

The windmill is Fenney Windmill and is a listed building.

Go along the road for just over ½ mile until you reach a footpath sign on the right, just after the power lines cross the road, at a place which is called Botany Bay. Perhaps this is where the poachers of Poacher's Corner were sent!

10. Turn right on a broad track. At the end of the lane, go ahead through the iron gate. The path crosses the eastern end of Blackbrook Reservoir.

Blackbrook Reservoir was constructed in 1796 in order to feed the Charnwood Forest Canal, which has long since vanished. The first dam constructed was an earthworks one, and this failed on 20 February 1799. In 11 minutes the reservoir was empty and as a result local farmland was ruined, sheep were drowned, and much of Shepshed and nearby Loughborough were affected by flood waters. The dam was repaired in 1801, but the canal was no longer commercially viable. The present gravity dam was constructed in 1906 and was officially opened by the first Mayor of Loughborough, Joseph Griggs. In 1957 the dam felt the effects of a magnitude 5.3 earthquake. The tremors caused heavy coping stones to shift and cracks appeared in the faces of the dam.

11. On the far side, go right through the kissing gate to walk in the field with the reservoir on your right. Go through a second kissing gate and turn left up the next field with a hedge on your left. At the top of the field, catch your breath and admire the view behind over the reservoir and the vista beyond. Bear right at the marker post and go through two kissing gates and ahead on a path climbing up in the woodland. Go through another kissing gate onto a road. Turn right.

In June 1935, a groom called Wood was leading two horses on this road past the Abbey gates when he saw one of the monks in a white habit standing by the side of the road. As he approached he saw the monk rise up the perimeter wall, glide over the top and disappear. The horse became extremely agitated, rearing and trying to bolt, and subsequently refused to pass that part of the Abbey walls.

Earlier that same day, a young monk, Brother Finbar Holland, had been working in the pump house, which was the other side of the wall, and had suddenly died. Sadly, Brother Holland had been due to be ordained a few days later and instead of attending his ordination his family arrived to find themselves attending his funeral.

Turn left on the access road to Mount St Bernard Abbey then left, following signs for the church and the car park.

WALK 12
NEWTOWN LINFORD
5½ miles

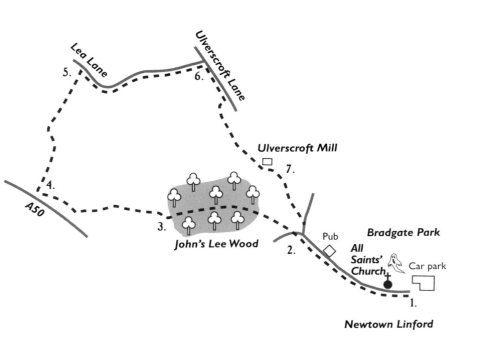

Lea Lane

Ulverscroft Lane

5.

6.

Ulverscroft Mill

7.

A50

4.

3.

John's Lee Wood

2.

Pub

Bradgate Park

All
Saints'
Church

Car park

1.

Newtown Linford

This is an enjoyable walk away from the crowds of Bradgate Park, through fields and woodland and country lanes. It is best avoided in mid-summer, when some paths may be overgrown with nettles and brambles, and after periods of heavy rain when it can be extremely muddy.

It may be combined with Walk 13 Groby by starting at Groby Pool Car Park.

Distance: 5½ miles
Grade: A
Parking: Newtown Linford Car Park, Bradgate Road. Pay and display.
Map ref: SK 522097. Explorer 246 Loughborough, Melton Mowbray & Syston and Explorer 245 The National Forest maps.
Pub stop: The Bradgate in Newtown Linford.

All Saints' Church is the destination of Bradgate's most famous ghost, Lady Jane Grey. She is said to set off from Bradgate House on Christmas Eve (other older versions say New Year's Eve) in a coach pulled by four black horses. She was described by one witness as dumpy. When she reaches the church she leaves the coach and the whole spectacle vanishes. She is said to reappear again nine days later and return to Bradgate House.

A woman cycling through the village late one Christmas Eve afternoon heard the sound of several horses in the vicinity, though she saw none.

A photograph taken on a family outing near the bridge with the churchyard in the background showed what appeared to be a monk among the gravestones. His blurred outline seemed to be wearing a dark habit.

He was not seen at the time the picture was taken and was only apparent when the film was developed.

ROUTE ---

1. Leave the car park by the entrance and turn right. Stay on this road for ½ mile, then turn left on Markfield Lane at a sign for the M1 and A50.

All Saints' Church, where Lady Jane Grey's ghost alights from its phantom coach.

2. After 100 yards, turn right over a stile at a public footpath sign for the Leicestershire Round. Follow the direction of the arrow in the field, going diagonally across to an iron gate in the corner. Go over the stile and ahead in the next field. Turn right at a kissing gate and cross another stile, bearing left at a sign 'Bailey-Sim Wood'. Go through an iron gate and ahead in the field with a hedge on your right. Continue through another iron gate and straight ahead, finally going through a wooden gate onto a lane and bearing left, following the yellow marker, through the open gateway.

3. Pass through the small gate and turn right with the hedge on your right. Go through two more gates and over two stiles, then turn right through an iron gate and turn left on the path. Cross a stile into the field to walk with a wood to your left. Where the wood starts to swing away to the left, leave it to keep ahead to a gate and yellow marker in the far end hedge. Go through the iron gate and bear left. When you see a yellow marker post ahead, bear right away from it to two unmarked wooden posts and a stile. Go over the stile and ahead on the path for ¼ mile until you reach a fingerpost on a lane.

4. Turn right to go through a kissing gate and head downhill and through a gate at the bottom. Continue ahead, going through a wonderful tunnel of trees. Pass two stiles on the right and go over a stone bridge, then through a kissing gate to cross the field with the hedge on your right. Go through four more kissing gates with the hedge/fence to your left to reach a road.

5. Turn right (Lea Road). Just past the thatched cottage follow the road round to the left. Stay on this quiet lane for ½ mile until you reach Ulverscroft Lane.

6. Turn right. After ¼ mile turn right at a public footpath sign for Newtown Linford, going over the stile and down the track. Follow the track round to the left. Go over a stile by a gate and bear left in the field, leaving the track, walking parallel to the hedge on your left. On the far side, go over the stile and ahead between trees. Stay on this meandering path, eventually crossing a grassy track and going ahead over a stile at a yellow marker post. Go over a bridge and go diagonally left in the field to reach the stile, which is 30 yards to the right of the corner and hidden by trees. Continue on a clear path, dropping downhill, with the ruins of Ulverscroft Mill on your left.

7. At the bottom of the hill turn left, then, after 30 yards, turn right over a stone bridge and ahead across the field. Go straight across two more fields then bear slightly left in the third heading for the houses, to a stile in the corner. Go up the gravel drive to the road and turn right, staying on the main road back to the car park. You pass the Bradgate pub on your left-hand side.

WALK 13
GROBY POOL
3½ miles

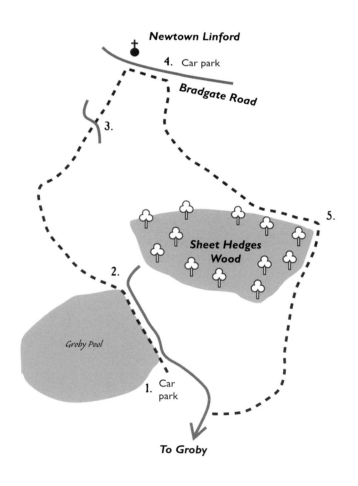

Newtown Linford

4. Car park

Bradgate Road

3.

5.

Sheet Hedges Wood

2.

Groby Pool

1. Car park

To Groby

This is an attractive shorter walk on good tracks and paths. It starts by the waterside of Groby Pool with its bird life, taking you to Newtown Linford with its coffee and tea shops, and returning over the fields. It may be joined to Walk 12 at Newtown Linford for a longer walk.

It is best avoided after periods of heavy rain when some parts may be extremely muddy.

Distance: 3½ miles

Grade: A

Parking: Free car park near Groby Pool, ½ mile from Groby, on the Groby to Newtown Linford Road.
Open 1 April to 31 October 8am to 8pm. 1 November to 31 March, 8am to 4.30pm.

Map ref: SK 525080. Explorer 233 Leicester and Hinckley map.

Pub stop: None, but a choice of tea and coffee shops in Newtown Linford.

ROUTE -

1. Facing the entrance of the car park, bear diagonally left to leave it by the left-hand corner, turning left over a bridge and ahead on a paved path to reach Groby Pool.

Fishermen's tales abound about the size of the one that got away, but the 18-stone pike of Groby Pool is one that was landed!

In the 18th century, the Squire of Tooley Hall, Tom Tooley, enjoyed fishing, hunting and visiting his mistress in Groby Pool House. His wife knew nothing of his bit on the side and the Squire hoped that this would

Groby Pool, where an 18-stone Pike was landed!

continue. However, the vicar of Ratby decided that he would tell Tom Tooley's wife of the affair, even though he and Tom were friends. Nothing was mentioned when they next met, but a few weeks later the men went fishing on Groby Pool. Suddenly, Tom Tooley grabbed hold of the overweight cleric and tossed his interfering friend into the water. After leaving him to struggle for a few minutes, he relented and hauled the man, whose name was Parson Pike, back into the boat. Thus, an 18-stone pike was actually caught in Groby Pool!

There are also a couple of unusual local sayings in connection with Groby Pool. A retort to anyone bragging or showing off is 'I'll thatch Groby Pool wi' pancakes.'

Another, said when someone unpopular dies, is 'There'll be many a wet eye in Groby Pool today,' meaning that the only wet eyes will be those of the fishes!

Continue in the same direction, keeping the Pool on your left, returning briefly to the road and then back into the trees. The path meanders adjacent to the Pool for about ¼ mile. Then, where it returns to the road on a right-hand bend, turn left at a footpath sign through a kissing gate.

2. Go on a narrow path, which eventually becomes a track. Continue straight ahead on the track for about ½ mile, following marker posts. Follow it uphill as it swings right and left. Go over a stile by a gate and ahead for another ¼ mile to reach a road.

3. Turn right and immediately left over a stile at a public footpath sign. Go ahead, dropping down a field with a hedge on your right. Cross a stile and continue ahead on a narrow path to reach the road opposite the church and car park in Newtown Linford. Turn right.*

It is at this point that the walk can be joined to Walk 12 to make a longer walk. *If doing so, turn left instead of right at this point and use the instructions in Section 1 of Walk 12 starting at 'Stay on this road for ½ mile…' Then, at the end of Walk 12, return to these instructions at Section 4.

4. Pass the road called Bracken Hill, then turn right at a public footpath sign. Go over a stile by a gate and stay against the right-hand hedge to keep the farm on your left. Cross another stile and go through a small wooden gate and turn left. Then go into the field, following the direction of the arrow on a clear path through the crops. The path goes left on the far side with a hedge on your right. Pass a yellow marker, then at a second marker post and an open gateway, go into the next field and turn left, walking with the hedge now on your left. At the next arrow post follow its direction bearing right. On the far side of the field, go into the woodland and follow the yellow arrow sign and turn left. Go through a kissing gate into the field and ahead with the wood on your right. At the end of this field, go through the gate. Do NOT go over the stile on the right at this point. Instead, continue for another 30 yards to another kissing gate on the right.

5. Turn right and go down the field with the wood on your right. Go over a stile by an iron gate and straight ahead down the next two fields. Continue with a hedge to your right in the following field. When you reach a yellow marker post, turn right over the stile. Go over a footbridge bearing left, then turn right at an arrow post to walk with a hedge on your right to reach a road.

6. Cross over and turn right to reach the car park after 300 yards.

WALK 14
THORPE SATCHVILLE
7¾ miles

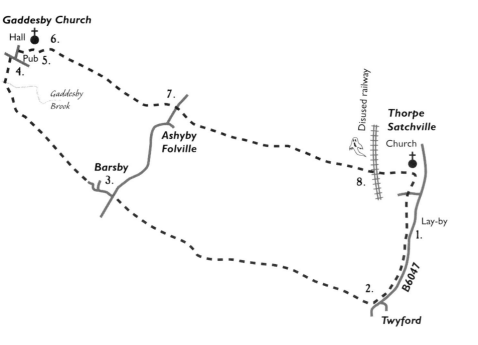

This is an enjoyable walk across the fields between the villages of Thorpe Satchville, Twyford and Gaddesby, where there is a beautiful parish church to visit. An ancient train and its passengers adds to the ghostly interest.

Distance: 7¾ miles

Grade: A

Parking: A lay-by on the B6047, midway between Thorpe Satchville and Twyford.

Map ref: SK 732110. Explorer 246 Loughborough, Melton Mowbray & Syston map.

Pub stop: The Cheney Arms, Gaddesby. Open lunchtimes every day except Monday.

ROUTE

1. From the lay-by, when facing the road turn left and continue for ½ mile, going through Twyford. Pass Main Street on the left, going onto Tilton Road, then, on a left-hand bend, bear right onto a lane with a bridleway sign.

2. Bear right onto a path between a hedge and a fence. Go over a stile and keep straight ahead, following yellow arrow signs across the next nine fields. In the 10th, bear right to follow the field boundary round to the left and ahead again in this field and the one after. Continue down a broad track to some farm buildings, going down steps to a lane and ahead to the main road in Barsby.

3. Cross over and go ahead on Main Street, continuing on The Lane. When you reach two signposts at a farm, turn right on a broad path following the bridleway sign. Go over a stile and follow the direction of the arrow in the field, bearing diagonally right, passing the small clump of trees and pond to your right. Continue in the same direction in the next three fields. In the fifth field, turn right to the yellow marker post and a stile, 30 yards from the corner. In field six, pass between the grassy mound and the trees on your right to reach a wooden bridge over Gaddesby Brook. Bear left up a broad, tree-lined lane to reach the road.

4. Turn right. Your pub stop, the Cheney Arms, is on the left. Go past the pub and turn left on Main Street, signposted Rotherby and Kirby Bellars. Just before the gateway to The Hall, turn right on a public footpath signed 'Church and Ashby Folville' to reach St Luke's Church. Your route continues, bearing right at the war memorial, but take time to visit the church should it be open.

The Church of St Luke's dates back to the mid-14th century and it has connections with the Knights Templar of Rothley. The exterior is lovely with its ornamented buttresses and tower and broach spire. The interior is also beautiful and interesting and well worth a visit.

Inside is a near life-sized sculptured monument to Colonel Edward Hawkins Cheney of the Royal Scots Greys. It was done by Joseph Gott in 1848 and depicts Col. Cheney on one of the four horses that were shot from under him at the Battle of Waterloo in 1815. Col. Cheney had a distinguished military career of over 21 years and lived at Gaddesby Hall on retirement.

The sculpture is the only equestrian statue in an English church. The teeth of the horse have been stained by the apple which is placed in its mouth at harvest festival time. On completing the monument, Joseph Gott realised that he had unfortunately left out the tongue of the *in extremis* horse. Sadly, it is said that in despair of this omission, he committed suicide.

5. Bear right at the war memorial at the entrance to the churchyard and ahead on a path. At a road, bear left over a stile by an iron gate and ahead on a lane, passing between fences to reach a junction of paths.

6. Go over the stile to the right then take the left-hand of two paths bearing diagonally left across the field. Go over a plank bridge and left across the corner of the next field to a stile. Go onto the footpath and ahead in the field on a clear path. Go past the trees on your right-hand side and continue along the field boundary to a stile. Continue ahead in the second field then go over two stiles crossing a path. Follow arrow signs over the next six fields to reach a road.

7. Turn left and almost immediately right at a footpath sign for the Leicestershire Round and Thorpe Satchville. Follow the direction of the signpost across the field. Go down the garden, bear right across a lane and over the stile. Go straight across the next two fields. In field three, if the crops are high bear right then left along the field boundary, and continue ahead in field four adjacent to the hedge on the right, passing under the power lines. Bear right in field five, then, at the corner, go left for 20 yards and over the stile. Follow the direction of the arrow in field six. Cross the corner of field seven, then go diagonally left down the next large field to reach a yellow marker and a wooden gate. Go under the railway bridge.

In 1989, Mrs Marshall was taking her dog for a walk along the disused railway cutting near Thorpe Satchville. The tracks had long since been

Old railway cutting, where a ghostly railway scene appeared.

removed and grassed over and it was a favourite place to walk. But one summer evening she began to feel uneasy. Suddenly she saw a crowd of people standing by an old-fashioned train. The engine had a tall chimney and was much older than the steam engines of the 1950s. There were three or four carriages which curved in at the bottom.

The women were wearing crinolines and carrying parasols and the men were dressed in tail coats and breeches with stovepipe hats on their heads. There were children too and she could hear the sound of voices, but no one seemed to notice her.

After six or seven minutes the whole scene faded away. At the time, Mrs Marshall found the experience intriguing rather than frightening, but since then she has become uneasy about walking there. The dog, which originally did not seem disturbed at the railway scene, is now as reluctant as his owner to go there.

There have been other reported incidents on that section of line. A previously well-behaved horse threw its rider when he tried to ride it along there.

8. Go diagonally right across a small field and continue in the same direction, going diagonally left up the following field to reach a yellow post by a large barn. Continue over two stiles, then, with Thorpe Satchville church to your left, bear right in the field beyond and go through the iron gate. Walk down the next field and up the other side. Go over a stile and straight ahead, crossing a paved lane to another stile. Bear diagonally left down this large field, heading for a road that may be glimpsed below, to a stile in the bottom left corner leading on to the road. Turn left to the lay-by.

WALK 15
STAUNTON HAROLD
9 miles

Melbourne
Pool

7.

Pub Wilson

6.

Golf Course

Staunton
Harold
Reservoir

To Melbourne

The
Coppice

Spring
Wood

8.

5.

9.

1.

Car park

Laundry Pond

2.

Dimminsdale

B587

Staunton
Harold Hall

3.

Lay-by

4.

This is a pleasant undulating walk through fields and woods set to the south and east of Staunton Harold Reservoir.

Distance: 9 miles
Grade: A/B
Parking: Car park at the southern end of Staunton Harold Reservoir.
Map ref: SK 378220. Explorer 245 The National Forest map.
Pub stop: The Bulls Head, Wilson. Open lunchtimes and weekends.

ROUTE -

1. Leave the car park by the entrance and turn left down the hill. Cross the end of the reservoir, then halfway up the hill turn left at a sign for Dimminsdale Nature Reserve. Go ahead on a clear path and down the steps to a pond.

Your route lies to the right, but go across the footbridge to the left, as it is worth pausing for a moment at this pond, which is the haunt of a kingfisher and is covered in dragonflies in summer. It is called Laundry Pond and was originally a quarry for lime kilns, which are now buried in its depths. There has been limestone quarrying in this area since 1300.

The area is called Dimminsdale, which is thought to be derived from Demon's Dale. However, there do not seem to be any stories to explain this and it may be that the glow of the fires of the lime kilns looked ghostly and evil in mediaeval times.

The pool is called Laundry Pond because a knoll overlooking the pool is the former site of a cottage, which was the laundry for Staunton Harold Hall.

Return from the pond and go ahead past the bottom of the steps, passing a second pond on the right. Climb up a hill and, at the top, turn right through a gap stile marked Ivanhoe Way. Keep straight ahead through the wood then go over a stile into a field and continue with a hedge on your left. Where the hedge swings left and you see a road ahead, bear right to the road. Turn right, then when you reach another road, turn left.

2. After 150 yards turn left at a sign for the Ivanhoe Way on a lane. Pass a public footpath sign to the right, then turn left at a yellow arrow post through an iron kissing gate. Go ahead for two fields with a fence on your right. Go through another kissing gate and down the field with the hedge on your left, then through a third kissing gate in the bottom left-hand corner. Continue ahead with the hedge/woodland now on your right for two fields. Follow the direction of the arrow in the following field. On the far side bear right on a lane.

Through the trees to the left you can glimpse the imposing building of Staunton Harold Hall. It has a strange story attached to it, set in 1760. On 18 January Dr Thomas Kirkland was travelling home with a companion when he had two extraordinary visions. Firstly, he saw himself giving evidence in a murder trial at the House of Lords, something he could not imagine ever coming to pass. Secondly, when he had stopped at a stream to water his horse, he saw an elaborate funeral procession go past. There were six black horses drawing an ornate carriage, on the side of which was the coat of arms of the Ferrers family. When he remarked on it to his companion, he was amazed that his friend had seen nothing of the cortège.

As soon as Dr Kirkland reached home he was summoned by Laurence, Earl Ferrers, to come immediately to Staunton Hall. Earl Ferrers was a cruel man with a temper which bordered on the insane. His previous violent acts had culminated on this day in him shooting a steward to whom he had taken a dislike. The man died the next morning and the Earl was arrested and confined in the Tower of London. Dr Kirkland gave evidence at his trial, fulfilling his first vision, and the Earl was sentenced and hanged at Tyburn. His funeral procession was spectacular and took three hours to pass due to the number of spectators, thus fulfilling the doctor's second vision from four months before. Earl Ferrers was the last peer to be executed for murder in this country.

3. Where the road swings left, at a yellow arrow post, leave it and go straight ahead through a small wooden gate by the side of a large five-bar gate on a green lane. Keep straight ahead, passing a footpath to the right at a yellow marker post, continuing until you reach footpath signs to the right and left.

Staunton Harold Hall, which has two strange visions associated with it.

Turn left through an iron gate, then, just before the outbuilding, turn left then right at the next arrow post. Follow its direction to the next yellow post. Go over the stile into the lane. Turn right, then, after 30 yards, turn left over a stile and follow the direction of the arrow sign up the field. Go over two stiles to reach a road.

4. Turn left. Stay on the road for ¼ mile until you reach a public footpath sign on the right, opposite a lay-by for parking. Turn right here and follow the direction of the arrow across the field. Cross a narrow field, then walk with the hedge on your right for two fields. At the bottom of the second field, turn right over a stile and go ahead for two fields with the hedge on your left. In the third field continue with the hedge on your left, but when you reach a yellow arrow post on the left, go through the hedge and turn right and continue now with the hedge on your right to reach a lane.

5. Turn left, then, after 50 yards, turn right. Cross the field with the hedge on your left, then, at the end, turn right before the gateway following the arrow sign, staying in the same field, still with the hedge on your left. Remain adjacent to the hedge on the left following the yellow posts. Continue ahead on a broad grassy path. When you emerge into a field, walk with the hedge on your left.

Where the hedge juts into the field, go through a gap passing a yellow marker post hidden behind the hedge. Continue in this field now with hedge on the right. When you come to an open gateway and a yellow arrow, return to walk on the other side of the hedge so that it is on your left again. Follow the broad track when it swings left and then right and continue ahead for another ¼ mile, reaching a tarmacked road and passing Breedon Priory Golf Club. As you approach a T-junction, turn left at a yellow arrow post over a stile. This is just before the sign for Park Farm.

NB: If a pub stop is required, go straight ahead onto the road and the Bull's Head is on the right.

6. Follow the direction of the arrow, going diagonally left up the field. Go over the stile at the top and then down the next field with the hedge on your right. At the bottom of the field go ahead on a broad stony track and then on a lane.

7. Turn left at a footpath sign where you see Melbourne Pool ahead. Go straight ahead across two fields, then continue with a hedge on your left in the third field. Turn left when you reach steps and a yellow marker. Go over a stile and ahead, now with a fence on your left. Continue on a cart track under trees. Where you reach a wood on your right and the track drops down and goes left, leave it and go ahead over a stile. Keep ahead adjacent to the wood on your right. At the end of the wood go straight ahead to a stile, then bear left to a yellow marker post and on to a carved gap stile.

In the fields to the left, you may see an unusual breed of cow — black with a wide band of white around their middle, rather like Liquorice Allsorts on four legs! These are Belted Galloways and they are a hardy breed originating from the exposed uplands of Galloway in the south-west of Scotland. They are long living, regular breeders, noted for producing rich milk and therefore rearing a good calf.

8. Turn right on this permissive path with the hedge on your right. Follow the hedge as it bends left and right, then turn right at a yellow arrow sign through another gap stile with 'Our pared' on it.

There are words on each side of this stile and the next six. See if you can work out what the phrases are. I warn you that for one set you are doing it in reverse!

Go through a kissing gate and continue adjacent to the hedge on your left-hand side. Go over the stile onto the road and then bear left across the road to a stile on the far side.

9. Go into the woodland, through another stile and left at the yellow arrow. Continue on this clear path until you reach another stile with 'Legs pass' on it and a yellow arrow where you turn right. Go over a stile with 'Give us' on it, then turn left at a yellow arrow on a broader path. Turn right on a path which is 30 yards before a wooden gate at another arrow sign to eventually reach a road. Cross straight over to another stile.

Did you work out the phrases? The two sayings are:
    'There's nothing worth the wear of winning but laughter and the love of friends.'
    The reverse phrase is:
    'Our pared legs stand [meaning the stile's] to let your paired legs pass. Give us your hand.'

Go straight ahead in the field with the hedge on your left. At the end of this field go into the next one and turn immediately right (not signed) to walk with the hedge on your right. At the bottom of the field turn left to the yellow post and right through the stile. At a yellow arrow, bear left down the steps and continue descending to reach the car park.

WALK 16
BELVOIR
7 miles

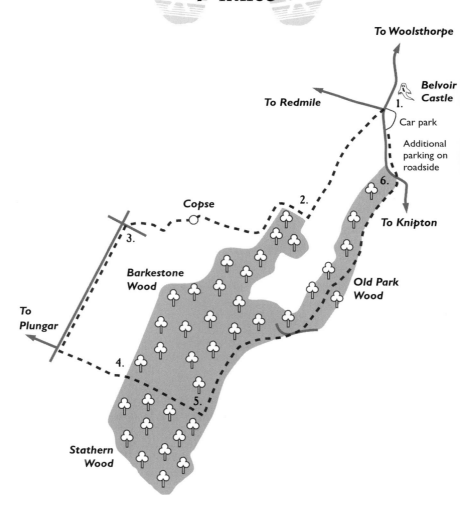

To Woolsthorpe

Belvoir
Castle
1.

To Redmile

Car park

Additional
parking on
roadside

Copse

2.

6.

To Knipton

3.

Barkestone
Wood

Old Park
Wood

To
Plungar

4.

5.

Stathern
Wood

In this walk you visit the most northerly point of Leicestershire, starting from the historic Belvoir Castle. It is an enjoyable excursion through fields and broad-leaved woodland, with one steep hill and spectacular views over the Vale of Belvoir. A ghostly highwayman needs to be avoided when driving in the area!

Distance: 7 miles

Grade: A/B

Parking: Belvoir Castle car park or on road side as far as SK 816328 (Knipton Road.) The walk starts at Belvoir Castle car park, which is at a T-junction where the Redmile Road joins the Woolsthorpe to Knipton roads. However, if this car park is not open there is parking on the roadside on the Knipton Road. The walk rejoins the Knipton Road and returns along it.

Map ref: SK 817337. Explorer 260 Nottingham Vale of Belvoir map. Belvoir Castle opening times: March and April – limited opening, May to August – open every day except Fridays, September – open Saturdays and Sundays only, between October and March – mainly closed except for specific events.

Pub stop: None.

The first Belvoir Castle was built on this site in the 1080s by Robert de Todeni, who was Standard Bearer to William the Conqueror at the Battle of Hastings. The present castle is the fourth to stand here since Norman times. George Manners was created 1st Earl of Rutland in 1525 by Henry VIII and the 9th Earl was created Duke of Rutland in 1703.

Therefore Belvoir has been the home of the Manners family for 500 years and the seat of the Dukes of Rutland for over three centuries.

The 6th Earl of Rutland is buried in the Church of St Mary the Virgin at Bottesford in what is called the 'witchcraft tomb'. An effigy of Francis lies between his two wives, Frances and Cecilia, with his sons kneeling at the base of the tomb holding skulls. Part of the inscription states that his two sons died in their infancy 'by wicked practice and sorcerye'.

This relates to an alleged witch, Joan Flower, and her two daughters Margaret and Phillipa. The three were known as the Belvoir Witches and were disliked and mistrusted by all who knew them, including the Countess Cecilia, the second wife of Francis. Margaret Flower was employed at the castle as a poultry maid and laundress, but when she was caught stealing food she was dismissed on the spot. However, this incurred the wrath of the three women and Joan Flower is said to have sought revenge on the Earl's family by sorcery.

It is said that they began casting spells upon the 6th Earl and his family and soon afterwards Francis and his wife Cecilia became sick and suffered 'extraordinary' convulsions. Although they recovered, their son Henry then fell ill and died, followed by their second son Francis who also died, seven years after his brother. The evil three then turned their devilish practices upon the daughter, Katherine, but she recovered.

The women were finally arrested and at the trial Joan Flower is said to have called for bread and butter, saying that if she were guilty of witchcraft God would strike her dead as she ate. She took one bite and immediately choked to death. This affirmed her guilt, together with her daughters', and the women were hanged in Lincoln Gaol on 11 March 1618.

ROUTE --

1. With your back to the Belvoir Castle car park, at the junction of the roads to Woolsthorpe and Knipton, walk down the Redmile Road for 20 yards and turn left at the footpath sign. Pass through the small wooden gate and bear right, following the direction of the sign, to go over a stile by the side of a double five-bar gate. Go ahead on a broad grassy track and continue for a mile until you reach a wood.

2. Turn right on a narrow track (not signed) on the edge of the wood, to walk with the trees on your left. On the far side of the wood, at a yellow sign, turn left. Continue for about ¼ mile to another marker post where you turn right. Follow the direction of the arrow across two fields. On the far side of the second field turn left, then after 50 yards, turn right. Go straight through the copse and follow the arrow sign in the following field. Bear right across the corner in the next field. Go over the stile and turn left, with the hedge on your left, then, when you reach a yellow marker, turn right across the field. Go slightly left in the remaining two fields to reach the road.

3. Turn left, following the sign for Plungar and Harby. Stay on the road for about 1 mile until you pass the road to Plungar. Then, after another 30 yards, turn left at the footpath sign to walk with the hedge on your right for two fields.

4. Go over a stile into the wood. At the marker post ignore the path to the right and keep straight ahead. Continue ahead at the yellow marker at a crossroads and again at the next unmarked crossroads. The path, which is

Belvoir, where you must beware a ghostly highwayman.

marked with yellow posts, climbs uphill becoming steeper and narrower and eventually reaching a T-junction and a level path.

5. Turn left. At a junction of paths after about ½ mile, keep right following the blue arrow. When you join a road after another ¼ mile, turn right, then after 100 yards turn left at a sign for the Jubilee Way and Bridleway to Belvoir. When you come to a cottage after ¾ mile, go straight over a lane and continue ahead for another ½ mile until you reach the road.

6. Turn left. This is the road to Knipton, where some of you may have parked. The road leads back to Belvoir. It is possible to walk on the grassy area on its right-hand side to avoid walking on the road, and you eventually reach the car park at Belvoir Castle.

In 1994, Dave Burrows had left the car park at Belvoir Castle and was driving along this road when he saw a figure standing by it. It was a man in a grey coat, who appeared to be hovering above the ground though his lower legs could not be seen. As Dave drew near the man stepped into the path of the car. Dave braked as the figure slowly vanished. He stopped the car and searched but there was no one to be found.

Other earlier reports describe a highwayman on a horse, who waits by the road before moving into the path of the car just as it reaches him. Strangely only the driver of the vehicle sees him. So take care if you are driving back by this route!

WALK 17
GARENDON PARK
4 miles

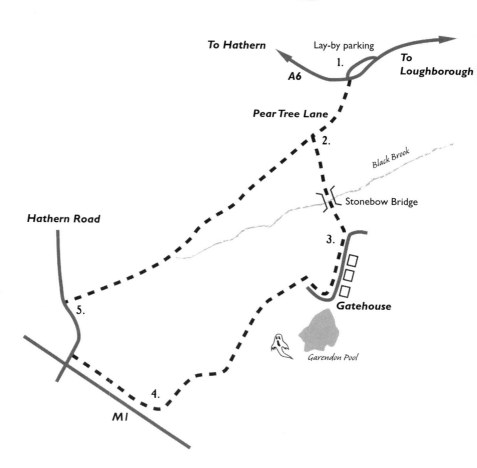

To Hathern

Lay-by parking

1.

To Loughborough

A6

Pear Tree Lane

2.

Black Brook

Stonebow Bridge

Hathern Road

3.

Gatehouse

5.

Garendon Pool

4.

M1

This is an easy walk between Loughborough, Shepshed and Hathern on tracks, through fields and woods. The strange tale of the blood-red Garendon Pool adds to its interest.

This walk may be linked to Walk 18 Hathern to make a longer walk.

Distance: 4 miles

Grade: A

Parking: A large lay-by on the left-hand side of the A6 when travelling from Hathern to Loughborough. It is about ½ mile from Hathern and is opposite an unsigned track called Pear Tree Lane.

Map ref: SK 509211. Explorer 245 The National Forest Map.

Pub stop: None.

ROUTE -

1. Facing the main road, leave by the right-hand end of the lay-by. Turn left and cross over the A6 at the central reservation then turn right on the other side. Note the old mile post with 'London 111 miles' on it. After 30 yards turn left up a track marked 'Bridleway to Shepshed 2'. This is called Pear Tree Lane. Pass a white cottage, then go ahead through a gate, continuing ahead on a paved track.

2. When you come to a yellow marker post, go left through a kissing gate and down through the woodland. Go over Stonebow Bridge, which crosses Black Brook, and go ahead. Ignore a footpath to the left for the Thorpe Acre Trail and continue until you reach a road with a wall in front of you.

Garendon Pool, which turned blood-red during the Civil War.

3. Turn right and continue along the road with the wall and buildings on your left.

At the end of the buildings you will see the only remaining gatehouse for Garendon Hall, which was pulled down in 1964. The Hall was built on the site of a 12th-century Cistercian abbey. Garendon Pool may be glimpsed to the left by going 50 yards into the field beyond the gatehouse. Note this is not public access.

In 1645, during the Civil War, the water of the pool turned red. Over the next four days the colour deepened and the water became thicker and more viscous, so much so that the surface no longer rippled in the breeze.

Some locals dipped cloths in it, dyeing them deep red, and kept them as good luck charms.

Later, great lumps of what seemed to be congealed blood began appearing on the surface and sinking down again. After four days the colour faded and the pool returned to normal. In an effort to explain the mystery, the pool was drained and a layer of 'blood' was found to line the whole of the bottom of the pool. However, throughout this experience, the fish were completely unharmed.

No explanation has ever been found to explain this phenomenon, which was reported widely at the time. The four days that it lasted were attributed to God's anger at the bloodshed of the four years of the Civil War. The fact that the water cleared was taken to mean that peace would once again return.

Your route continues on the paved lane which turns right opposite the gatehouse. When you come to a yellow marker after 200 yards, turn left. Go past a gate and continue ahead on this broad lane for ¾ mile.

4. When you reach the bridge over the M1 do not go over it. Instead, turn right down steps and ahead across two fields with the M1 to your left, continuing to a road. Turn right and stay on the road for ¼ mile.

5. When you reach a yellow marker, with a sign 'Bridleway to Loughborough', turn right. Keep straight ahead. Pass under power lines, then, in the next field, keep the brook on your right. Halfway along the following field turn right through the gate and then left, with the hedge on your left. On the far side of the field, go through the large gate and ahead on a tree-lined avenue and then continue on this clear track until you reach the road opposite the lay-by and parking.

WALK 18
HATHERN
6¾ miles

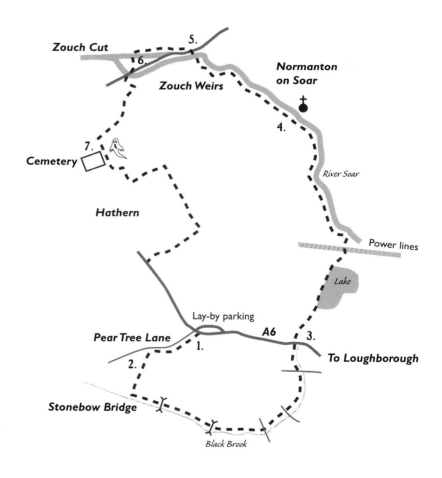

Zouch Cut

5.

6.

Zouch Weirs

Normanton
on Soar

4.

7.

Cemetery

River Soar

Hathern

Power lines

Lake

Lay-by parking

Pear Tree Lane

A6

3.

1.

2.

To Loughborough

Stonebow Bridge

Black Brook

This is a most enjoyable flat walk in an area to the east of Hathern, taking you through woods and then by the side of Black Brook and continuing along the River Soar.

Distance: 6¾ miles

Grade: A

Parking: A large lay-by on the left-hand side of the A6 when travelling from Hathern to Loughborough. It is about ½ mile from Hathern and is opposite an unsigned track named Pear Tree Lane on the map.

Map ref: SK 509211. Explorer 246 Loughborough, Melton Mowbray & Syston map.

Pub stop: None.

ROUTE

1. Facing the main road, leave by the right-hand end of the lay-by. Turn left and cross over the A6 at the central reservation then turn right on the other side. Note the old mile post with 'London 111 miles' on it. After 30 yards, turn left up a track, marked Bridleway to Shepshed 2. This is called Pear Tree Lane. Pass a white cottage then go ahead through a gate, continuing ahead on a paved track.

2. When you come to a yellow marker post, go left through a kissing gate and down through the woodland. When you reach a stream at Stonebow Bridge, go left before the bridge, and walk with the water (Black Brook) on your right. Duck under a bridge! Then, after passing a second bridge, go down some steps and bear left on a tarmacked path on Blackbrook Way. Pass

Morrison's supermarket and continue with the brook on your right. Cross three roads.

3. Pass under a fourth road (A6), then after 100 yards turn right on a tarmacked lane with playing fields to your left. After 300 yards, turn right over a bridge. (Note a mobile snack bar is available at this point on Saturdays and Sundays.) On the far side of the bridge, turn left at the yellow arrow post to walk with the brook on your left. Keep straight ahead at a bridge and junction of paths, continuing for about ¼ mile, passing a lake on your right. Pass under power lines, then turn left on a grassy track, to have the River Soar on your right. Continue for ¾ mile on a clear path by the river.

4. Pass the church, houses and moorings of Normanton on Soar, staying by the river. When you reach a sign 'Danger Weir. Keep Right' continue for 30 yards then turn right and cross over three bridges over the weirs to reach the road.

5. Turn right, then, after 30 yards, turn left at a public footpath sign. At a second sign keep left with the water of Zouch Cut on your left-hand side. When you come to a bridge at a crossing of paths, turn left, crossing the bridge, and then keep ahead in the field beyond to reach a road.

6. Turn right. Cross the river then turn left at a yellow marker post. Bear left to a second yellow marker post. Go over a stile and ahead on a track for 100 yards. Just before an open gateway, turn sharp right to pass under the power lines and ahead to a marker post. Go over a stile and bear right across the corner of the field to another yellow marker. Go over a wooden bridge and ahead up the field with the hedge on your right. At the top of the field at another yellow marker, turn left, continuing with hedge on your right, then onto a track to pass the cemetery.

It was on a spring afternoon in 1988 that Mrs Myra Hurt was walking her dog, Tiny, along this lane past the cemetery. When she saw a boy on a bicycle approaching, she picked up her dog and waited for him to pass. To her amazement the boy and bike disappeared before her eyes! Thinking about it she realised that the bicycle had been an old-fashioned upright model and the boy had been dressed in short grey trousers and a pale shirt, not in the modern teenage wear of today, and this led her to wonder whether she had seen a ghost.

Hathern cemetery, haunted by a ghostly cyclist.

She decided to check the headstones in the graveyard to see if anything matched. The only one she found was of a boy named Freeman, aged 14. By asking in the village, Myra found that the Freeman boy had indeed been killed while riding his bicycle and therefore concluded that it was his ghost that she had seen.

A strange rider to this tale is that, although she has searched the cemetery many times since, she has never again been able to find the grave of the Freeman boy.

7. Continue to the road. Turn left then bear right at the bottom on The Green, then go left on Pasture Lane on a byway. Pass the Hathern C of E primary school, then, after another 200 yards, turn right at a public footpath sign. Go down the field with the hedge then a fence on your right. At the end of the fence, go ahead through the small iron gate and bear right to continue in the next field with the hedge on your right. Where this hedge ends, turn right at the marker post, continuing with a hedge on your right. Bear right at the end onto a lane and ahead to the main road. Turn left on the road to walk the ½ mile back to the lay-by and parking.

WALK 19
THRINGSTONE
1 or 3 miles

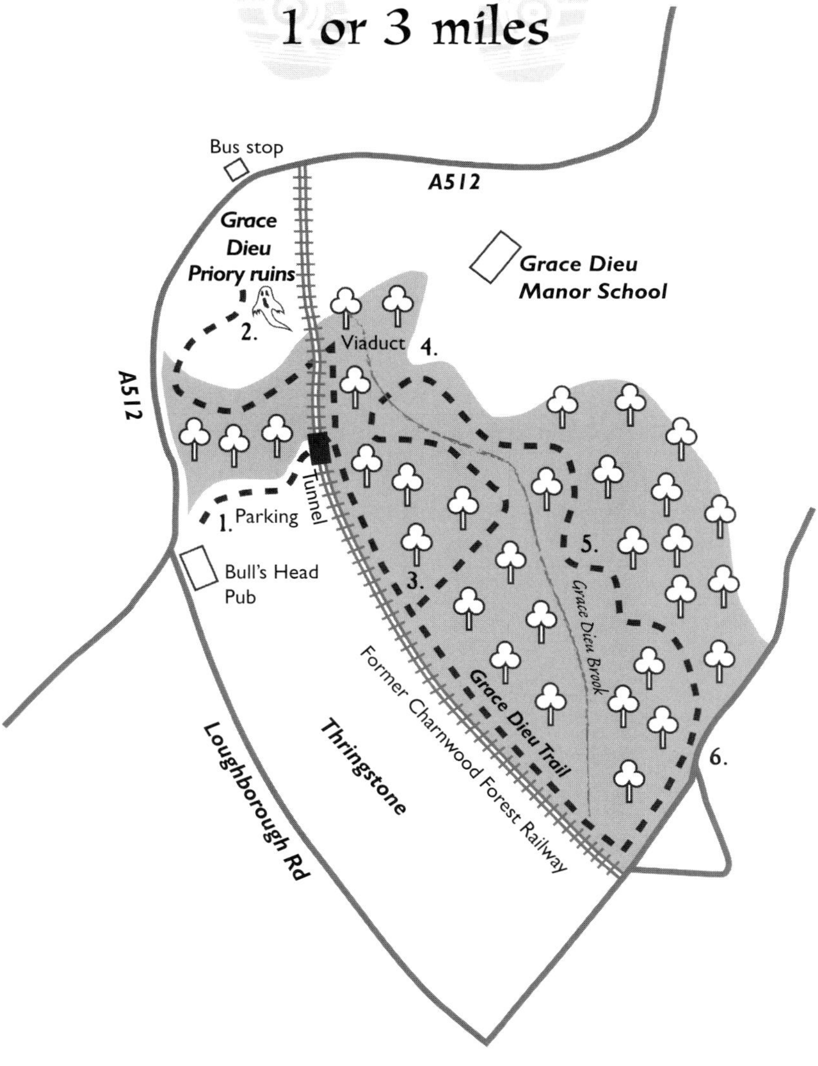

Bus stop

A512

Grace Dieu Priory ruins

2.

Grace Dieu Manor School

Viaduct   4.

A512

Tunnel

Parking
1.

Bull's Head Pub

3.

5.

Grace Dieu Brook

Grace Dieu Trail

6.

Former Charnwood Forest Railway

Loughborough Rd

Thringstone

A visit to the ghostly ruins of the 13th-century Grace Dieu Priory and an easy woodland stroll gives you the choice of a pleasant one-mile or three-mile walk.

Distance: 1 or 3 miles

Grade: A

Parking: Car park at rear of Bull's Head Pub in Thringstone, which is at the junction of Loughborough Road and the A512 Ashby to Shepshed road.

Map ref: SK 431181. Explorer 245 The National Forest map.

Pub stop: The Bull's Head. Open every day from 12 o'clock.

ROUTE —

1. With your back to the pub, leave the car park by the top left-hand corner going onto the Grace Dieu Trail. Go down a path to reach a tunnel under the former Charnwood Forest Railway. Go through the tunnel and turn left. Continue ahead then bear left under the viaduct. Turn right when you reach a five-bar gate marked 'Access to Grace Dieu Priory.'

These ruins and the surrounding area must be one of the most haunted areas in Leicestershire judging by the number of ghostly sightings. Grace Dieu Priory was founded in the 13th century by Roesia de Verdun as an Augustinian religious house for nuns and was occupied until its Dissolution in 1538. Many of the reports which span the last 80 years are specifically of nuns or of figures dressed in white, which was the colour of habit that these nuns wore.

Grace Dieu Priory, the scene of many supernatural sightings.

As early as 1926, a carriage passing the ruins was brought to a halt when its horse shied as six figures in white robes crossed the road and moved into the ruin.

Motorists driving on the A512 road have had many strange encounters when passing the ruin in the area of the bus stop and the lane which leads to Belton. In 1954 a bus driver stopped to pick up a woman in white but no one got on. The conductor and driver left the bus and searched but found no one. Again, in 2002, a bus driver saw a figure near the bus stop and slowed to pick her up, but the figure vanished.

More frightening was Denis Baker's experience, when at the same spot a woman stepped into the path of his car. He braked but heard no impact, and in his rear-view mirror he saw her carrying on across the road.

Two motorcyclists in the 1980s had encounters at this point. One, a police constable, noticed the temperature plummet then a grey shrouded figure passed in front of him. In 1986, Vince Ball saw a white luminous figure crossing the road. Both he and the car in front stopped and confirmed what they had seen.

Within the ruins, a council worker engaged in improvement work, having seen the figure of a woman watching him, received a push in the back. Other visitors have been pushed and footsteps have been heard on the plank staging on the scaffolding.

One explanation of the figure of the woman on the road is that it is the ghost of Roesia de Verdun, the founder of the priory. She died in 1247 and was buried in its chapel. During the Dissolution her remains were removed and reinterred at Belton church. As so many of the sightings are in the region of the lane to Belton, it is thought that the nun is trying to express her wish to have her remains returned to the priory.

2. Return by the same route, turning left after the five-bar gate and bearing right at the viaduct. When you reach the tunnel on your right, you can return to the car park. Alternatively, for an additional two-mile walk, continue past it. When you reach a footpath sign, turn left, signed Grace Dieu Wood.

3. Keep straight ahead, ignoring a path bearing left. Cross a path and go through a wooden gap stile. On reaching another path turn left, with Grace Dieu Brook below you to the right. Continue down to the stream. Go through another gap stile and turn right.

4. Keep straight ahead through a gap in the fence, then 20 yards after a yellow arrow, turn right at a crossing of paths. Cross the lovely stone bridge over the brook, then, at a sign for Grace Dieu Manor School, turn right on a permissive path, with the brook on your right-hand side. The path meanders but remains clear.

5. Further on you enter a woodland grotto, a clear area under three fir trees. The path here bears to the right over a semi-fallen tree. At a second grotto, pass the knobbly tree to your right and continue ahead past the one leaning left. When you return to the brook, the path bears left, almost hiding itself under holly trees.

Go straight ahead across another woodland grotto under fir trees, with higher ground to the left of you. On the far side, bear left up a short rise, ignoring a fork to the right at this point. You emerge onto a broad path. Turn right and continue ahead as the path swings right through a more open area. Cross a narrow path and keep straight on over a second path. Go straight over another fir tree glade. Cross a final path then go left to reach a road.

6. Go right and then, after 30 yards, turn right again and go down the lane. Just before the main road, turn right by the side of an iron gate on the Grace Dieu Trail. Remain on this tarmacked path, crossing the brook then keeping straight ahead for ½ mile until you reach the tunnel on your left. Turn left here back to the car park.

WALK 20
FRISBY-ON-THE-WREAKE
8 miles

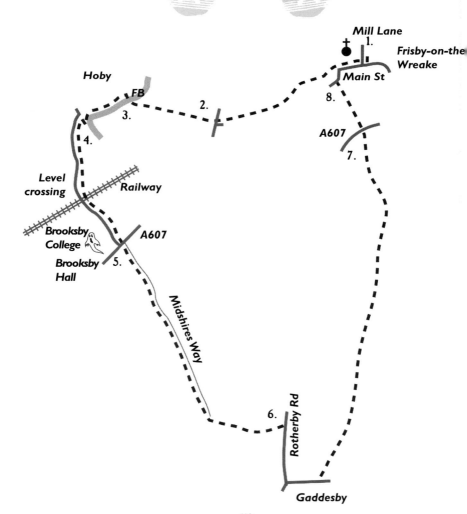

Mill Lane

1.

Frisby-on-the-Wreake

Hoby

Main St

8.

FB

2.

3.

A607

4.

7.

Level
crossing

Railway

Brooksby
College

A607

Brooksby
Hall

5.

Midshires Way

6.

Rotherby Rd

Gaddesby

This is a pleasant and well-signed walk set to the west of Melton, circling the villages of Frisby-on-the-Wreake, Hoby and Gaddesby. It is through fields and on tracks and roads and has lovely open views. It is best avoided in autumn, when ploughing will make crossing some fields difficult.

Distance: 8 miles

Grade: A

Parking: Mill Lane, Frisby-on-the-Wreake, at the back of the church and cemetery. Additional parking may be found on Main Street, down which you will travel at the beginning and end of the walk.

Map ref: SK 696178. Explorer 246 Loughborough, Melton Mowbray & Syston map.

Pub stop: The Bell Inn at Frisby-on-the-Wreake. Open Tuesday to Saturday 12–2pm and 6–11pm, Sundays 12–3pm and 7–10pm.

ROUTE --

1. Facing the cemetery on Mill Lane, go left up the road. When you reach the end of Mill Lane, turn right on Main Street. Continue until you reach the Bell Inn, where the road goes left. Leave the road and bear right between The Limes and Corner Cottage on a gravelled drive, signposted 'Leicestershire Round, Hoby 2 miles'. Continue between walls and through a kissing gate into the field. Keep straight ahead across five fields. Go through two metal gates and continue in the same direction for three more fields to reach a lane.

2. Cross over and follow the footpath sign to 'Hoby', bearing diagonally left down this large field to reach a yellow marker in the bottom left-hand corner. Cross the railway then bear left in the field beyond and follow the direction of the arrow for two fields.

3. Cross the bridge over the River Wreake. Go ahead to a yellow arrow post and follow signs to the left. Go through the kissing gate. Ignore the yellow arrow pointing right. Instead, bear left to walk with the river on your left-hand side as it winds right and left. Go over a second bridge and continue to the next yellow arrow. Leave the path at this point, turning sharp right up the field, with the hedge on your right. When you reach the water trough turn left, staying parallel to the fence at the top of the field to reach a yellow marker post and kissing gate onto a road.

Brooksby Hall, haunted by a 'White Lady'.

4. Turn left. Stay on this road for about ¾ mile, going over a level crossing and climbing a hill past the buildings of Brooksby Agricultural College. Just after a right-hand bend you reach the main gates and have a good view of the former Brooksby Hall.

Brooksby Hall is said to be haunted by a ghost called 'The White Lady', referred to as Lady Caroline. Its origin is thought to be linked to the finding of a skeleton by workmen in 1891–92. They knocked out a wall to install water tanks and found the gruesome sight of the skeleton of a woman and a baby. There were playing cards scattered over the floor. The bones were placed in a chest, a grave was dug by the blacksmith and a vicar conducted a service. Strangely, the funeral took place at night.

In the 1940s, the Hall was used to house wounded soldiers and people from nearby villages used to visit them. Diane Barnsley from Hoby was in the Great Hall one day when she saw a white mist on the wide staircase. It gradually took the form of a grey lady who glided down the stairs, approached the main door and vanished. A passing soldier asked 'What's up? Have you seen a ghost?' And she replied 'Seen one? I very nearly was one!'

She also saw the apparition of a coach and four horses driving away from the Hall one night. She saw both these ghosts many times after that, but says she was never frightened after that first time.

The sound of the rattling wheels of the coach and the galloping horses was also heard within the Hall, each time a few days before Christmas and at midnight. The coach appeared to stop, a heavy object was unloaded and then the coach moved on.

Although it is many years since sightings of the ghosts have occurred, there is one room within the Hall where both staff and students report waking in the night with the strong feeling of being watched. Could it be the one where the woman's remains were found?

Continue to the main A607 Melton Road.

5. Cross over using the central reservations to your right and go down the narrow lane on the opposite side towards more buildings of the Brooksby Melton College. Stay on the lane, bearing right at the marker post. Go through one iron gate then at the Spinney Dairy go through a second and continue ahead on a track. Where the lane emerges into a field, continue ahead with the hedge on your right for four fields. Go along a green lane with hedges either side. Ignore a stile and footpath to the right in the following field and pass through one more to reach a road.

6. Turn right. Go down the road for ¼ mile. When you reach Pasture Lane, turn left. After 300 yards turn left at a footpath sign for the 'Leicestershire Round Frisby-on-the-Wreake'. Follow the direction of the arrow signs across five fields.

Cross a lane and then continue ahead for two fields. Walk with hedge on left in fields three and four, then in five, head for the yellow marker in the middle of the end fence. Go over one small field and then up two more extremely large fields to finally reach a road (A607).

7. Cross over and turn right, then after 30 yards, turn left at a footpath sign for the 'Leicestershire Round Frisby-on-the-Wreake ½ mile'. Go ahead in the field with the hedge on your right to reach another road (Rotherby Lane). Turn right then bear right at the Bell Inn and go up Main Street. Turn left at Mill Lane back to the parking.

8. Turn right then bear right at the Bell Inn and go up Main Street. Turn left at Mill Lane back to the parking.

WALK 21
ROTHLEY STATION
3 miles

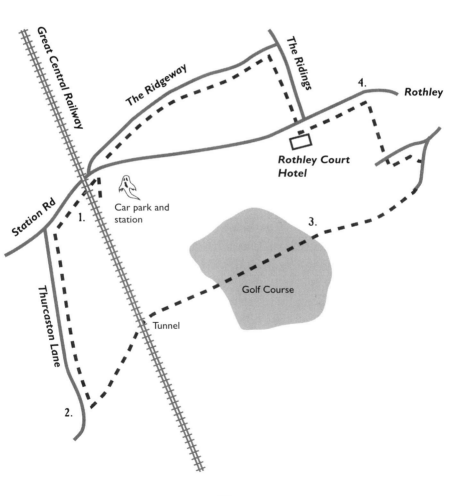

Great Central Railway

The Ridgeway

The Ridings

Rothley

4.

Rothley Court
Hotel

Station Rd

1.

Car park and
station

Thurcaston Lane

3.

Golf Course

Tunnel

2.

125

This is a pleasant easy walk on quiet roads, tracks and fields between the villages of Rothley and Cropston. Lovers of steam locomotives will enjoy its start from Rothley Station with its steam railway, restored buildings and a miniature railway.

Distance: 3 miles

Grade: A

Parking: Rothley Station car park. It is situated at the junction of Station Road and Swithland Lane, Rothley. (On the road from Rothley to Cropston.)
NB: The entrance to the station is on a sharp bend, opposite a post box and Swithland Lane, and access is down a narrow lane.

Map ref: SK 568123. Explorer 246 Loughborough, Melton Mowbray & Syston map.

Pub stop: No pub but Ellis's Tea Room is at the station. It is open every day except Friday from 10am to 3.30pm. It serves soup, jacket potatoes, paninis, sandwiches and cakes, as well as hot and cold drinks.

Rothley Station and its surrounding area have many reports of ghosts. Figures in Edwardian or Victorian dress have been seen by the stairs on the station, and a man and his dog have been seen both on the platform and on the line towards the Swithland signal box. The man was a farmer who used to take a short cut across the tracks in winter when the access road underneath became wet and marshy. He was warned against doing it many times by the Swithland signalman, but took to crossing at dawn and dusk so he would not be seen.

The line was a very busy one in olden days and eventually his luck ran out and he was killed by a passing train. In the years that followed railwaymen would often see his figure dashing across the tracks.

More recently a young man returning home late at night from a party in Mowmacre Hill decided to walk the three miles back to Mountsorrel on the railway tracks. As he came to Rothley Station, he saw a figure on the platform wearing a flat-topped cap and some sort of uniform, leading the young man to think it was a Station Master or porter. The figure appeared to be waiting for a train.

Rothley Station, haunted by many ghosts.

However, as he drew closer he was overcome with dread and fled across the sidings. He was sufficiently disturbed by the encounter to ask at the station later whether trains ran at night, and I am sure it did not help his peace of mind to learn that they did not!

ROUTE —

1. Leave the car park by the access road and return to the main road. Turn left, then, after 300 yards, turn left down Thurcaston Lane. Go down the road for ½ mile, going under power lines and crossing Rothley Brook. Then, just before the houses, turn left at a public footpath sign.

2. Follow the direction of the post going diagonally across the field, continuing in the same direction in the following field to the far corner. Go over the stile and through the tunnel under the railway. From the stile on the far side, bear slightly left for 10 yards to pick up a (hidden) yellow marker on the left. Follow its direction across the golf course. The route goes straight ahead and is signed (though somewhat sparsely) with yellow markers. It follows a line of trees for the most part.

3. On reaching the far side of the course, go over the stile and keep straight ahead for three fields then cross a stile into a lane. Turn left, then, after 50 yards, turn left across the green and then left again on the lane beyond. At the end, just beyond Keeper's Cottage, turn right at the footpath sign and go over a stile. Follow the fence on your left to reach a stile onto the road.

4. Turn left.

The Rothley Court Hotel is situated on a site with a long history. It was mentioned in the Doomsday Book of 1086, but prior to that a Roman villa existed in this place. In the 13th century the Knights Templar built their chapel here and it still stands today next to the current Manor House. The hotel's coat of arms is that of the celebrated Babington family, who held Rothley Temple and its surrounding land for nearly 300 years from 1550. The motto, which translates as 'Faith is all' was repeatedly said to Henry V on the eve of the Battle of Agincourt in 1415 by Thomas Babington, a squire on his personal staff.

Opposite the Rothley Court Hotel, turn right on The Ridings. When you reach the road called The Ridgeway, turn left. At the end of The Ridgeway, cross the road, bearing left to return down the access road to the car park.

WALK 22
MEASHAM 1
4½ miles

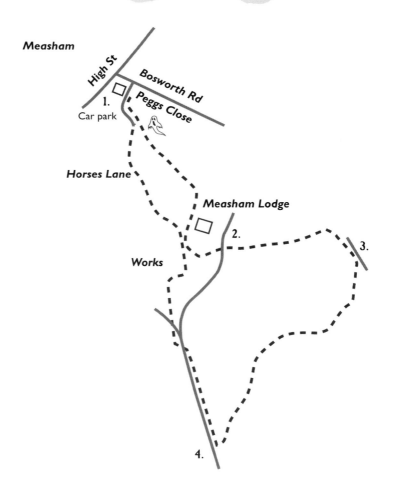

Measham

High St

Bosworth Rd

1.
Car park

Peggs Close

Horses Lane

Measham Lodge

2.

3.

Works

4.

This is an easy walk to the south of Measham on good paths. It may be joined to Walk 23 to make a longer walk.

Distance: 4½ miles
Grade: A
Parking: Free car park on Peggs Close, off Bosworth Road, Measham.
Map ref: SK 335121. Explorer 245 The National Forest map.
Pub stop: None.

ROUTE --

1. Leave the car park by the entrance and turn right. At the end of the road, bear left on to Horses Lane. Where the lane goes right, leave it to go ahead on a public footpath.

Many years ago, George, a resident of Peggs Lane, was taking his dog Pip for a walk late one night. He headed for the canal which used to be in this area, intending to cross it and walk along Horses Lane. As he reached the bridge he heard a splash, and when he shone his torch on the surface he could see ripples in the water.

When he tried to walk on, Pip refused to move and he realised that the dog was shaking. George shone the torch again, trying to see what was upsetting the dog, and saw a woman coming along Horses Lane towards the stile, which led to the towpath on the other side of the bridge. George crossed the bridge but when he lit the towpath there was no one to be seen. He checked the stile, wondering whether the woman had become stuck there, but to no avail.

Peggs Lane, where a tragic spirit still roams.

George managed to coax Pip over to the stile and instructed him to 'Find!' Reluctantly, the dog went along Horses Lane for about 80 yards to a small hawthorn bush on the canal bank, where he stopped. However, there was still no sign of the woman so George gave up the search.

A few days later, when George was relating the incident to Mr Burton, the local coal merchant, he learned that the little hawthorn bush on the bank was where a local woman had thrown herself into the canal and drowned.

Cross an open area then go over a stile into a field. Walk with the hedge on your right for two fields. Bear right and then straight ahead through the vehicles at Measham Lodge to pick up a yellow marker post at a gateway. Go ahead in the field adjacent to the fence on your left. Go left over a stile in the fence and follow the direction of the arrow across the field to reach a road.

2. Cross over and go straight ahead in a large field to reach a stile and marker post. Go over the stile. As the arrow indicates, the right of way goes along the hedgerow to your right. This was impassable at the time of writing. If this is still the case, go straight ahead for 30 yards then make your way to the right towards a portacabin. Go between the picnic tables. Do NOT go down the steps. Instead, turn left at the top of them on a cleared path to walk with the hedge on your right, which is a continuation of the blocked footpath.

The churned up area to your left is due to 'Have a go at off-road Tank Driving!'

At the end of the path bear left to a bridge and a road.

3. Turn right, then, after 100 yards, turn right at a yellow marker and stile well hidden in the hedge. Go ahead on a narrow and then broader path on the top of an embankment for about ½ mile. Then turn right at a yellow marker at an open gateway and follow the direction of the arrow, bearing left to 10 o'clock across the field. On the far side, turn left to walk with the hedge on your right. At the bottom of the field, continue ahead bearing left on a muddy track. Stay on the lane for ½ mile, going through the farmyard to reach a road.

4. Turn right. After nearly ¾ mile, when you approach the junction, take the left fork, signposted Measham. Then, as you go onto Atherstone Road, turn immediately right onto the Ivanhoe Way. Remain on this path as it winds around the perimeter of the works. Then continue on a paved path. When you reach a road, turn right over the bridge. Go left and then right up the road to return to the car park.

WALK 23
MEASHAM 2
5½ miles

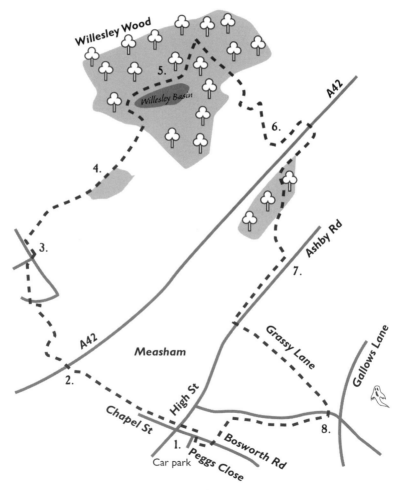

This is a pleasant walk set to the north of Measham, taking in Willesley Wood. It is mostly on good paths. It may be joined to Walk 22 to make a longer walk as both leave from the same car park.

Distance: 5½ miles

Grade: A

Parking: Free car park on Peggs Close, off Bosworth Road, Measham.

Map ref: SK 335121. Explorer 245 The National Forest map.

Pub stop: None.

ROUTE

1. Leave the car park by the entrance and turn left. At the end of the road, turn left again on Bosworth Road. At the T-junction with High Street, turn left and immediately right on Chapel Street. Continue to the end of the lane then go through the kissing gate into the field. Cross the field with the hedge on your right. On the far side pass the first marker post and stile and continue round the end of the field for 30 yards to a second yellow marker.

2. Turn right and cross the bridge over the A42 and continue on the other side, still with a hedge on your right. Where the path divides, stay adjacent to the hedge. Go through a small gate and continue in the same direction in the following field. On the far side, turn left at the marker post and go down the field. When you reach the houses, turn right through a kissing gate and ahead to a road. Turn left, then, after 50 yards, turn right at the white railings, keeping them on your left. Continue ahead on a cycle track to reach a road.

3. Turn right then left at the main road. After 100 yards turn right at the public footpath signed 'Willesley Wood ¾ mile'. Go over the stile and straight ahead. On the far side of the field, go down the steps and follow the direction of the arrow, to reach a marker post near the barns. Continue ahead with the hedge on your left. The path passes close to a small lake and after heavy rain small sections of it become submerged. If this is the case, it is necessary to make one's way through the denser undergrowth. However, the path soon improves and becomes passable again.

4. Go over a stile. Ignore both of the arrows. Instead, go straight ahead to walk with the hedge on your right. Keep straight on where a path joins from the left. Then, at a T-junction and yellow arrow, turn left. As the path starts to climb up a hill, leave it and head for a marker post across a broad grassy area, with the water of Willesley Basin to your right. There are benches along this stretch and it is a pleasant place for a break.

5. Continue to the far end of the lake, ignoring paths to the left. Bear left, passing a bench dedicated to John Ludlam Bullen, Air Crew Bomber Command. Bear left again at a junction of paths and head for an iron gate. Just before the gate, turn right on another grassy path. At the top of the rise, at a yellow marker post, turn right and then take the left-hand fork. At a T-junction turn left, then turn right before a second iron gate, turning left at the top of the hill to a stile by a third iron gate.

6. Go over the stile and bear left on a lane, then cross the A42. Turn right on the far side. Pass a lane to the left and go down the hill. Go left at a yellow marker on a grassy path through the trees. When you reach a broad track, turn left and continue to a road (B5006 Ashby Road).

Gallows Lane, where a ghostly miner still rides his bicycle.

7. Turn right. Go down the road for ¼ mile, then 50 yards before the 30mph limit sign, turn left at house No. 65, going through a kissing gate to the left of their wrought iron gates. Go up the drive and ahead on Grassy Lane. Continue on this broad path for ½ mile until you reach a road.

Many years ago, washing-machine engineer Dave Lindsay stopped at the crossroads which you see to the left of you. To his left he saw a cyclist approaching, heading towards the village of Measham, which is to your right. The man wore a flat cap and gabardine mackintosh and had what looked to be a miner's 'snap' box on his handlebars.

The man was travelling very slowly and Dave waited impatiently for him to pass. As soon as he had crossed in front, Dave rechecked that the road was clear to the left and glanced to the right again. To his astonishment there was no sign of the cyclist. Concerned that the man had had an accident and toppled into a ditch, Dave left his van and searched the area but found no sign of him.

Over the next few days, Dave related his experience to everyone he met and was told by a number of people that his ghostly cyclist was most likely an old miner who had been killed in a road accident some 30 or 40 years before.

8. Cross over and turn right for ½ mile. Turn left at a short road called The Lakins, continuing on a narrow path to reach a road. Turn right and then left back to the car park.

WALK 24
NEWTON BURGOLAND
5½ miles

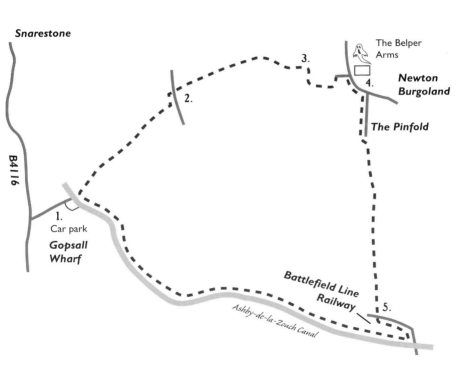

This is a pleasant easy walk on tracks and fields, finishing along the Ashby Canal, with the added interest of a ghost called Five to Four Fred! NB: Some field paths may be overgrown in summer.

Distance: 5½ miles

Grade: A

Parking: Gopsall Wharf, on the Ashby Canal. Access is from the B4116 about ¾ mile south of Snarestone.

Map ref: SK 347083. Explorer 245 The National Forest map.

Pub stop: The Belper Arms, Newton Burgoland. Open 12 until 12.

ROUTE --

1. Leave the car park by the entrance but turn right on the access road. Cross the bridge over the canal and go straight ahead on a track. Stay on this deeply rutted, and therefore muddy, track for nearly ¾ mile until you reach a lane.

2. Turn left, then, after 100 yards, turn right at a yellow marker post and stile. In the field go right and then left, to walk with the hedge on your right for two fields. Just before the end of the second field, go over a stile and turn left to walk with the hedge now on your left.

3. When you reach a yellow marker, turn right across the field to a stile. Go straight over a lane and through a wooden gap stile on the far side. Stay adjacent to the hedge on your left, following it round the end of the field. Turn left at a yellow arrow, crossing a bridge over a stream and ahead on a path. When you reach a road, turn left, then, after 50 yards, turn right at a footpath sign, bearing right to reach the main road. Turn right to continue the walk. Your pub stop, the Belper Arms, is opposite.

Parts of the Belper Arms date back nearly 700 years to when it was a cottage accommodating stonemasons working on Swepstone Church. Prior to this, the site was a knackers yard with a well for collecting blood situated at the rear of the pub. The body of a murder victim is said to have been deposited in the well.

The oldest parts of the building are the favoured haunts of the pub's ghost, called Five to Four Fred because of the time that he manifests, either in the morning or afternoon. Fred has never been seen or heard, but most certainly he has been felt, as Fred is a very tactile ghost with a preference for the ladies.

The Belper Arms, the haunt of a tactile ghost called Five to Four Fred.

Women feel his cold hands stroking their faces and a few have had a pat on the bottom. However, Fred does not seem to like men and they have reported feeling his hands closing over their mouths with the sensation of being smothered, the effect only being relieved by them leaving the pub. Both phenomena are preceded by a drop in temperature.

4. Coming out of the pub, turn left along Main Street. Just before the telephone box, turn right down the road called The Pinfold. At the end of the houses where the road bends to the right, leave it to go straight ahead on a narrow lane. Then, where the lane goes to the left, go over the stile to keep straight ahead on a public footpath. Leave the lane as it curves right to the house, going ahead on the grassy path. Go over a stile by a gate, passing a pond to the left, then go through a copse. On the far side, continue ahead with the hedge on your left for two fields, then with the hedge on your right for one field. Go straight across a final field to reach a lane.

5. Turn left. Go past the entrance to the Battlefield Line Railway on your right. Climb the hill and turn right on the road. Cross the bridge, then, just after the 30mph limit sign, turn right down the steps onto the canal towpath, following the sign for Snarestone. Stay by the canal for two miles, passing under three bridges. Then, at the fourth bridge, go up the steps to the right and through the gate. Turn left to cross the bridge over the canal back to the car park on the other side.

WALK 25
DONINGTON LE HEATH
4½ miles

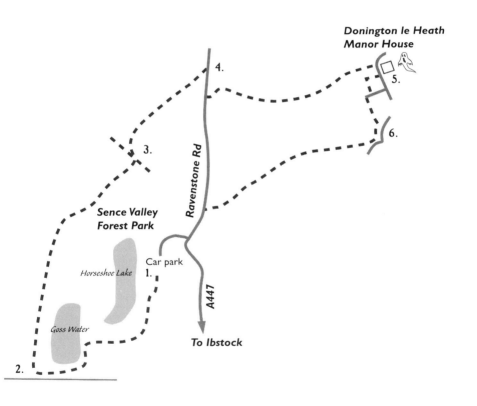

Donington le Heath
Manor House

4.

5.

6.

3.

Ravenstone Rd

Sence Valley
Forest Park

Car park
1.

Horseshoe Lake

A447

Goss Water

2.

To Ibstock

This is an easy walk between Ibstock and Coalville, utilising the Sence Valley Forest Park and a visit to the beautifully restored Donington le Heath Manor House, one of the oldest houses in England. NB: Some paths may be overgrown in summer.

Distance: 4½ miles

Grade: A

Parking: Sence Valley Forest Park car park on the A447 Ravenstone Road, north of Ibstock. Free parking and WCs. Note closing times when parking.

Map ref: SK 403113. Explorer 245 The National Forest map.

Pub stop: No pub, but the Classics Tea Rooms at Donington le Heath Manor House is open seven days a week, 11am to 4pm for most of the year. However, it is advisable to check times December to February for Tea Rooms and House.

ROUTE

1. Leave the car park bearing right on a path at the opposite end to the entrance. Go right by the zig-zag fencing, then turn left on a broad path, going down the hill with the lakes to your right. Pass Horseshoe Lake, then when you reach Goss Water, turn left keeping close to the water on your right. Follow the road round to the right, to the metal gate, where there is access left to the road.

2. Turn right over the stream and go ahead between fences. Continue for ½ mile, passing a path to the right to reach a footpath sign. Bear right, crossing a stone bridge and ahead on a track. Pass a footpath to the right, then, after

30 yards, turn left at a yellow arrow post. Go over the stile and turn right, to walk with the fence on your right.

3. Go over a stile onto a track and turn left up the hill. At the top, turn right over a stile taking the right-hand of two paths. Go down the field with a fence on your left. Bear right before the pools, heading for a yellow marker post. Go over the stile and follow the direction of the arrow in the field. When you reach a yellow arrow at the corner of the fencing, turn left to go up the field with the fence on your right, ignoring a stile at this point. At the end of the field, go over the stile and ahead on the path to reach a road.

4. Turn right, then, opposite the house, turn left at a bridleway sign. Go through the gate and ahead on a clear track for ½ mile. As you pass under the power lines, go left and immediately right in the field, with the hedge on your right. When you reach the houses, keep straight ahead on the lane. At the main road turn right. Donington le Heath Manor House is on your left.

The Manor House was built in the 13th century by Robert de Herle and remained a family dwelling for nearly 700 years. It fell into disrepair in its latter years when rented out as a tenant farm until 1963, when it was recognised as an ancient monument. Its restoration took seven years, and finally in 1973 it was opened as a museum.

There are a number of ghosts associated with the building, although sightings are said to be rare. Fleeting glimpses have been caught of a housemaid. Also there are reports of a man in 17th-century dress wearing a tall, brimmed hat. Some claim this to be the ghost of Sir Everard Digby, who was involved in the Gunpowder Plot. He did not live at Donington but is thought to have been a regular visitor.

Donington le Heath Manor House, where you may hear the ghostly crunching of gravel.

At a ghost-watching evening the sound of a child crying was recorded in King Dick's bedroom, although the watchers heard nothing at the time.

The most common phenomenon is the crunching of gravel on the south-west path as though someone is walking along it and stopping at the old stables. This has been heard by the gardener and the Museum Support Officer.

5. Leaving the Manor House, turn left down the road. Turn right on Holts Lane, then left at a footpath sign between Nos. 17 and 19. Turn right on the road, then, after 100 yards, turn left at a public footpath sign. Go down the field with a hedge on your left. Bear right at the bottom over the footbridge then left between the hedge and fence to reach a road.

6. Turn right and go around the corner past the remains of the bridge over the road, then go right over the stile at the side of the iron gate. Go ahead for four fields with the hedge on your right. Then, in field five, go diagonally left, heading for a marker post in the end hedge, 100 yards from the top left-hand corner. Go diagonally across the next two fields, then bear right on a track to reach the road. Turn left and then right into Sence Valley Forest Park and parking.

WALK 26
COSSINGTON–WANLIP
9 miles

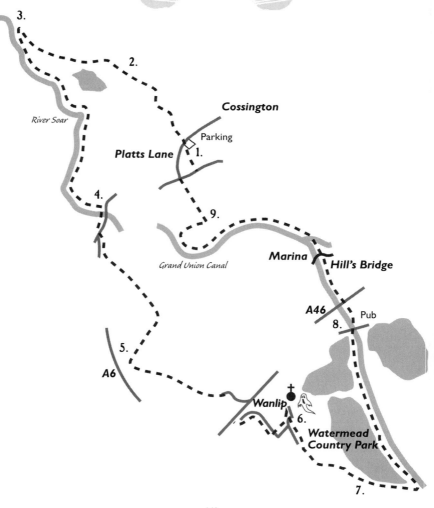

3.

2.

Cossington

River Soar

Parking

Platts Lane   1.

4.   9.

Marina

Grand Union Canal   **Hill's Bridge**

A46   Pub

5.   8.

A6

Wanlip   6.

Watermead Country Park

7.

This is a lovely 'water' walk, taking in Cossington Meadows, the River Soar, Wanlip Meadows, Watermead Country Park and the Grand Union Canal. It is on good paths and has a wonderful variety of scenery and wildlife.

Distance: 9 miles

Grade: A

Parking: Recreation ground on Platts Lane, Cossington.

Map ref: SK 603132. Explorer 246 Loughborough, Melton Mowbray & Syston map.

Pub stop: The Hope and Anchor, after Watermead Country Park, 6½ miles into walk.

ROUTE --

1. Leave the car park by the entrance. Turn right and almost immediately left at a footpath sign. Go through a kissing gate and ahead across two fields. At the end of the second field, bear right through the iron gate at the yellow arrow post. Continue ahead on a winding path then, at a junction of paths, turn left before the multiple arrow sign. (There is a choice of two paths which converge further on.) Go through a kissing gate and ahead at an information board for Cossington Meadows. Continue to follow the arrow signs, going straight over a wide track.

2. At the next arrow post go right, heading for the water to walk with the lake on your left-hand side. At the end of the lake go through a wooden kissing gate and continue straight ahead. Where the paths divide, take the right-hand one, keeping straight ahead until you reach the River Soar.

3. Turn left to walk with the river on your right. Stay by the river for 1½ miles. When you approach a bridge with four arches over the river, ignore a white arrow pointing left and instead go ahead to a yellow marker post and continue up to a road.

4. Turn right over two bridges then turn left at a yellow marker post and footpath sign on a broad track. Just after a gateway bear left to a kissing gate and go ahead on a narrow path, then with a hedge to your left for two fields. In the third field turn right at a yellow marker post, reached ¾ of the way along it. Follow the direction of the arrow, bearing diagonally left over the field, with the radio mast to your right, continuing on a broad track.

5. Just before the busy A6 road, at a yellow marker post, turn left between hedges. Continue for ½ mile. When you reach an access road, go ahead then turn right at a road signed A6, A46 west and Wanlip. Go left through the bridge under the A46 then left again on Fillingate signed Wanlip. Continue on Rectory Road. Turn left on Church Road, signed Wanlip Parish Church, left again at the T-junction and left to the church.

The churchyard has a seat for you to take a break, and should the church be open, its lovely interior is well worth a visit.

The Church of Our Lady and St Nicholas, Wanlip, dates back to the 14th century. There is a beautiful brass in the floor of the chancel depicting a knight and a lady as the founders of the church with an inscription dated 1393.

The church has a ghostly organist. John Ward, the church warden, was working in the church tower one day when he heard noises in the church below. He went down but found no one. When this happened a second time he checked that the church was empty and then locked the door, leaving the

Wanlip Church, where a ghostly organist plays.

key in the lock so that no one could enter. On returning to the tower he then heard the organ being played. He says he switched on his radio at this point! His wife Julie said that their dogs frequently refuse to go into certain parts of the church or bristle and stare at some places. The boiler room is an area that they particularly dislike.

The Ward's two daughters have also asked their parents where the man in the church has gone when neither John nor Julie has seen anyone.

Another ghost story associated with Wanlip occurred on a foggy night in 1989 when Cliff Lewis was driving carefully through the village. Suddenly the figure of a young black boy appeared in front of the car. Cliff braked but knew that he must have hit the child. He rushed from his car, fearing the worst, but there was no one to be seen. There wasn't a body lying in the road nor an injured child on the verge. He called out but there was only silence.

The next day he returned to the village. No one had heard of an accident the night before, but when he described the black boy he received some

The tomb of Rassalas Morgan, whose ghost still roams the village.

perplexed looks and was directed to an Egyptian-style tombstone in the churchyard. It lies on the left of the path between the graves of the Cullings family and that of Morton Lester.

Its lettering is worn now but it reads:

'Sacred to the memory of Rassalas Morgan, who was born in Macadi in the confines of Abyssinia and died at Wanlip Hall, 25 August 1839 in the 19th year of his age. Rescued from a state of slavery in this life and enabled by God's Grace to become a member of His Church. He rests here in the hope of a greater deliverance hereafter. This stone is raised in remembrance of his blameless life by one whom he loved.'

Rassalas is thought to have been one of the first slaves to be freed in Victorian England, although it is not recorded how he came to be employed by the Palmers of Wanlip Hall.

Nor is it known why his ghost should be walking the streets of Wanlip on a foggy November night in 1989.

6. From the churchyard gate, go straight ahead then turn right at the T-junction. Keep straight ahead on the road, going onto a track. At the end of the track go through two gap stiles then right on a broad path. Go through an iron kissing gate and go diagonally left, passing a pond to your left to reach a yellow marker post. Continue along the river as it winds left and right.

The sculpture which you can see ahead is on a platform in King Lear's Lake, the largest lake in Watermead Country Park. The legendary king is said to have built the city of Leicester and to have been buried in an underground chamber beneath the River Soar. The sculpture depicts the final scene from Shakespeare's King Lear.

Cross a small bridge then go ahead and left over the bridge over the river.

7. Turn right, signed Canal Street and Thurmaston. At a junction of paths and a notice board for King Lear's Lake, turn left on a paved path to walk with the lake to your left. Just before the path starts to rise, go right at a yellow arrow post through a kissing gate and then turn left to walk with the Grand Union Canal on your right.

> The Grand Union Canal stretches from London to Birmingham and is 137 miles long with 166 locks. It has arms to Leicester, Slough, Aylesbury, Wendover and Northampton.

WCs are available along this stretch.

Stay on this path for a mile until you reach a bridge. Turn right, crossing the bridge over the canal, then on the far side turn left back on to the towpath to walk with the canal now on your left.

The Hope and Anchor pub is situated here.

8. Stay on the towpath for ½ mile, passing under the A46 and under Hill's Bridge and through the marina. Go across a bridge and turn left, still with the canal on your left. Continue for another ½ mile, passing a weir and a lock. Then, after a long right-hand bend, where the canal starts to swing left, go over an unusual metal stile and turn right, heading for the cottage in the distance and a yellow marker at a gate. This is the left-hand one of two gates.

9. Turn left to walk with a lake on your left and go ahead to reach a road. Turn right then after 200 yards turn left at a footpath and yellow marker. Go straight through the wood and continue across the field to return to the car park.

WALK 27
WYMONDHAM
9 miles

Crown Point Farm

8.

7.

6.

Cribbs Meadow Nature Reserve

Disused railway

5.

Woodwell Head Wood

9.

Railway embankment

10.

Windmill

Berkeley Arms

1.

2.

Wymondham

4.

◇ Park Cottage

× Water pump

3.

† Edmondthorpe Church

This is an enjoyable walk to the south and east of Wymondham with numerous points of interest. It is mainly on tracks and bridleways, and although it returns across the fields, wide paths have been left by the farmer.

Distance: 9 miles

Grade: A

Parking: Limited. On Main Street, Wymondham.

Map ref: SK 851188. Explorer 247 Grantham, Bottesford and Colsterworth map.

Pub stop: None. However, the Windmill on Butt Lane has a tearoom which is well worth a visit. It is closed on Mondays and its opening times are: Easter to September, Tuesday to Friday 10.30am to 4.45pm. Saturday, Sunday and Bank Holidays, 10am to 5pm. October to Easter, Tuesday to Friday 11am to 2.30pm. Saturday, Sunday and Bank Holidays, 10.30am to 4.30pm.

ROUTE

1. The walk starts from Church Lane, which is opposite the Cottage Stores and the Berkeley Arms pub. Go down the lane, through the churchyard and out of the kissing gate. Bear right onto another lane and continue on this to reach a road. Cross over onto Wright's Lane. Where this lane bends left, leave it at a footpath sign to go ahead on a path between hedges. Cross a bridge over a stream and continue.

2. Where the path forks, go right onto a rutted track. Go through a wooden gate and ahead in the field with the hedge on your right. Go through an iron gate on a path through trees. When it emerges into a field, bear left to continue on a broad path between hedges. Where a path crosses your own, turn right then continue in the field with the hedge on your left, going ahead on a broad path between hedges. Then, 30 yards before the end of this path, turn left through an iron gate at a yellow marker post. Follow the direction of the arrow across the field to reach the road and church in Edmondthorpe.

In the mid-17th century Sir Roger Smith lived at Edmondthorpe Hall with his second wife, Lady Ann. She was of Spanish descent and it is said that people feared her because they thought she was a witch and could read their innermost thoughts.

When she and Sir Roger returned from an extended trip to London, Lady Ann seemed to know that the servants had been spending the time while they were away in partying and dancing. The butler was summoned and was shocked to hear that Lady Ann was able to describe in exact detail all that had taken place, even though she had spoken to none of the other servants.

Some time later, the butler was discussing with the cook the fact that he had seen Lady Ann riding out alone at night in the moonlight and he and the cook speculated about what she might be doing.

Suddenly, a large black cat sprang at the butler from the window ledge and clawed at his face. The cook grabbed a meat cleaver and struck at the cat, gashing its left paw, causing the cat to drop to the floor and flee, leaving a bloody trail. They tried to follow it but it disappeared and, returning to the kitchen, the cook found it impossible to remove the bloodstains from the flagstone floor.

When serving dinner that night the butler noticed that Lady Ann looked pale and ill and then saw, to his horror, that her left arm was heavily bandaged. As he opened his mouth to mention the earlier event in the kitchen, she transfixed him with her dark hypnotic eyes and he found himself unable to speak of the incident to Sir Roger.

The Church of St Michael and All Saints houses an alabaster monument of Sir Roger Smith and his two wives. If the church is locked, the statues may be viewed through the window on the far side of the church beneath

The church at Edmondthorpe that houses the effigy of Lady Ann.

the tower looking down the length of the church. It is a three-tier monument with Sir Roger lying between his two wives. The lower effigy is that of Lady Ann and there is a red stain which spreads over her garments, apparently from her left wrist. And, two and a half centuries after the event, the bloodstained flagstone still could not be scrubbed clean and was taken up in 1919 and removed on the orders of the Countess of Yarborough, who occupied the Hall at that time.

3. From the churchyard, turn right. Go along the road for ¼ mile until you reach the Village water pump outside the Edmonthorpe Social Club. Take a moment to admire this ornate pump, which dates from 1856. Just beyond it, turn right on to Woodwell Head Lane.

The ruins of Edmondthorpe Hall may be glimpsed through the trees to the right. It was built by Sir Roger Smith in 1621. In World War Two it was used as a prisoner of war camp until it burned down in 1943.

4. Stay on this lane for ¼ mile then, 50 yards beyond Park Cottage, turn right at a yellow marker post on a broad track. Where the track ends, go straight ahead into Woodwell Head Wood. Go through the wood. On the far side, bear left, keeping the wood on your left. Then continue with a hedge on your left in this field and the following one, going onto a broad track, following it round a left-hand bend and past a yellow marker, still with the hedge to your left.

If there is the sound of engines over to the right at this point it is from the Harrier Jump Jets stationed at RAF Cottesmore. Although they are very noisy, drowning out the birdsong, they are an amazing sight as they practise their low flying and then halt in mid-air, hovering over the airfield.

5. At the next marker post turn right. At the end of the field, go left over the bridge, through the iron gate and turn right, to walk now with a hedge on your right for two fields.

You are now in Cribbs Meadow Nature Reserve. It was originally a glebe, a portion of land providing income, belonging to the Vicar of Edmondthorpe. The name comes from Cribb's Lodge and is in memory of the last bare-fist prize fight in England held in 1811 at Thistleton Gap, which is two fields south of here. The fight was between Tom Cribb and Tom Molyneux.

The fields are covered in many notable species of plant, including cowslips and orchids in spring and early summer, and the two ponds contain great crested newts.

6. Just before the end of the second field, turn left over a stile and climb the steps over the railway embankment and down the other side. Cross the field with a hedge on your right to reach a gate onto the road. Turn left, then, at the road junction, turn left again, signposted 'Wymondham and Melton'.

7. On a left-hand bend, turn right on a lane with sign for Bluepoint Horses (the marker post is hidden in the hedge and broken at the time of writing). Go past the farm and onto a grassy track, then bear left into a field. At the end of this field, go straight ahead on a track for 10 yards then turn left, following a blue arrow sign.

8. Go down this field and the following one with the hedge on your left. Continue on a path between hedges and then go straight across field three. Keep the hedge on your left in fields four and five, crossing a lane in between. Go straight across field six, with the hedge on your left for its remainder and in field seven. At the next arrow post turn right on a broad track to reach a road.

9. Turn right. After 300 yards, on a left-hand bend, turn left through an iron kissing gate at a public footpath sign. Go ahead in the field and through a second kissing gate to continue with the hedge on your right. At the next arrow post, at a junction of paths, go right across the bridge then left in the next field to walk with the stream that you have just crossed on your left. Go through an iron gate and straight ahead across the meadowland. On the far side, go through another iron gate at a yellow marker post and straight ahead. Go through a third iron gate and turn left to walk with a fence on your left.

As you turn a right-hand corner, the embankment to your left is the same disused railway line you crossed in the Nature Reserve. It was an LMS line (London Midland Scottish) which ran from the west from Melton Mowbray with links to Nottingham and Leicester. To the east it joined the Midland and Great Northern Line and ran to King's Lynn and on to Cromer and Great Yarmouth on the east coast.

Ahead you can see Wymondham Windmill, which dates back to about 1814 and is well worth a visit at the end of the walk. It is up Butt Lane, which is adjacent to the Berkeley Arms. It has a craft shop and tearooms serving a range of delicious cakes, scones and teacakes, as well as more substantial snacks and hot and cold drinks.

10. When you come to a marker post, turn left up some steps and over the embankment. Then go through a kissing gate and straight across the field to pick up a yellow marker post on the far side. Turn right on Main Street back to the start of the walk and parking.

WALK 28
TILTON ON THE HILL 1
10 miles

Tilton on the Hill

Garage

11.   1.
Parking
Digby
Close

2.
B6047

Old
Station

Hamners
Lodge Farm

Lowesby 10.

3.

Lowesby
Hall

9.

8.

4.

Wood

Baggrave
Hall

7.

South
Croxton

King's Lane

5.

New
Covert

Pub

Waterloo
Lodge Farm

6.

This is an excellent walk in an area known as High Leicestershire. It has extensive views and undulates through a wide variety of scenery, going through fields and green lanes, valleys and woods, between the villages of Tilton on the Hill and South Croxton.

Distance: 10 miles

Grade: B/C

Parking: Digby Close, off Leicester Road (opposite Tilton Garage), Tilton on the Hill.

Map ref: SK 742057. Explorer 233 Leicester & Hinckley and a small part on Explorer 246 Loughborough, Melton Mowbray & Syston maps.

Pub stop: The Golden Fleece, South Croxton.

The Saxon settlement of Tilton on the Hill is situated at the crossroads of two ancient paths that are thought to have linked Leicester, Oakham, Market Harborough and Melton Mowbray. At 700ft above sea level it is one of the highest parts of Leicestershire, and the spire of its ancient church, built around 900 years ago, can be seen from miles around.

The village, together with those of South Croxton and Twyford, had a reputation for witchcraft which persisted until the latter half of the 19th century. In 1875, Sarah, a witch who was the wife of a Tilton shepherd, was said to be able to transport herself to the local woods and cause a tree to burst into flames by using her wand.

Another witch from Tilton was Old Betty, who could cause blood to flow from a tree by striking it.

Old Joe of Twyford could bewitch farm implements so that no one could use them and cast spells on horses so that they were unable to work. Because of this Old Joe never had to labour himself, but instead lived on handouts from local farmers who paid to keep on the right side of him.

All the witches from the three villages were said to be killed when they were seen in the guise of cats, floating in a large wooden bowl on the brook at dawn. The villagers threw big stones at them, breaking the bowl and drowning the witches.

Tilton on the Hill, which had a reputation for witchcraft.

ROUTE ---------------------------------

1. Go out of Digby Close and turn left on Leicester Road. After 200 yards turn right on a road signposted Halstead and Loddington. Then turn right at the Rose and Crown, going onto Main Street. At a T-junction turn right, signposted Billesdon and Houghton, then at a road junction turn right again, still following signs for Billesdon and Houghton. Stay on this road for nearly ¾ mile to reach a main road (B6047).

2. Turn right, then, after 50 yards, turn left at a public footpath sign to Cold Newton. Go over the stile and straight across two fields. Continue in the same direction for ¾ of the way across the third field. Then, where there is a footpath to the left with red and white poles, turn right at a 90 degree angle across the field. When you reach a yellow marker post with a red arrow on the left, turn left to walk with a hedge on your left. Where the hedge ends, follow the red arrow sign, going onto a broad track dropping downhill. When you reach the farm, continue to follow the red arrow as the track winds down the hill. At the bottom of the hill it becomes a paved lane and starts to climb. Go through a gate and continue ahead.

3. When you come to a T-junction, turn right, then, after 50 yards, turn left through a gate following the sign for the Midshires Way. Go straight across the field to reach an iron gate in the left-hand corner. Keep straight ahead in the following field, ignoring arrows directing you to paths to the left and right, and continue to a five-bar gate. Go through the gate and turn left to go up the field with a hedge on your left. Follow the direction of the arrow sign in the next two fields.

4. At the end of the second field, follow the sign for the Midshires Way, going through the five-bar gate into the wood. Go straight through the wood. On the far side, continue between hedges, go across a drive and keep straight ahead on a wide track, still between hedges. When you come to a field follow the direction of the arrow bearing left. Go straight across the following field. On the far side of this second field, go straight ahead, leaving the Midshires Way at this point, to walk on a green lane. Go through two small gates onto the road and bear right. Then, after 500 yards, where the road goes right, leave it to go ahead on the public bridleway at a sign for Waterloo Lodge Farm.

5. As you approach the farm and reach a sign saying that this is not a legal route, turn left through the gate and immediately right, to walk with the hedge on your right (not signed.) Continue for 100 yards then turn right over the stile at the yellow marker post. Cross the lane and go through the gate on the far side. Bear slightly left in the field. Cross a stile at a yellow marker post and follow the direction of the arrow, bearing right to a marker post and a stile into the wood. Go through the wood and then straight across the field. On the far side, go over the stile and turn right to walk with the hedge on your right. At the next marker post, bear left following the direction of the arrow to reach a stile and marker post in the corner. Go ahead between hedges, cross a small field and follow the direction of the arrow across the garden. Then go left on the lane to reach a road.

6. Turn right. This is South Croxton. Your pub stop, the Golden Fleece, is on the right.

Just past the pub turn right on King's Lane. Continue for 50 yards beyond the end of the houses then turn right at a yellow marker post and footpath sign. When you come to a T-junction, turn left to follow the yellow marker post. Go straight across a field. Go over a stile and ahead on a path between fences, passing between pools.

At the next stile and a choice of paths, go right. At a marker post, follow the path round to the right. Then go through an iron gate and cross a bridge over Queniborough Brook. Go over a stile and bear left to walk parallel to the brook on your left, to reach a marker post and stile in the middle of the hedge at the far end. Keep straight ahead in the next field to reach a marker post in the right-hand corner. Go over a stile and straight ahead across the parkland of Baggrave Hall to reach a lane at a footpath sign.

Baggrave Hall is now a private mid-Georgian residence built on the site of an earlier Hall. Edwyn Burnaby (1798–1867) of Baggrave Hall was one of Queen Elizabeth II's great-great-grandfathers on the maternal side.

To your left at this point is the site of the mediaeval village of Baggrave, which was deserted in the 1500s.

Leicester Abbey owned 216 acres of land at Baggrave. In 1517 it is recorded that Abbot John Penny 'enclosed the messuages [dwelling houses with outbuildings and land], cottages and lands with hedges and ditches. The hamlet of Baggrave is laid waste and the people have departed in tears.'

7. Go left and then right through an iron gate at another public footpath sign. Go ahead for ¼ mile with a narrow lake/waterway to your right, eventually leaving it at an arrow post. Cross a bridge and go over a stile into a field.

8. Turn right to walk with the trees on your right. At the far end of this very large field, turn right through a gate and over the stile. Ignore the direction of the arrow. Instead, go straight ahead up the field to reach a stile which is 30 yards to the left of the right-hand corner. Go straight across the following field. Go down three steps and go diagonally left to a marker post on the corner of the wood and walk with the wood on your right. Where the wood ends, keep straight ahead to reach a marker post and five-bar gate. Continue straight ahead for the next two fields, going onto a track in the third field.

9. Cross a lane and continue in the same direction. As the imposing view of Lowesby Hall comes into sight, bear slightly left to keep the house and walled grounds to your right. A marker post on the end of the wall finally confirms that you are on the right path.

> The area to your left at this point was once the site of the mediaeval village of Lowesby. Lowesby Hall is connected to the Fowke Baronetcy, which was created in 1814 for Frederick Gustavus Fowke. There are many memorials to the Fowke family in the Church of All Saints, which you will pass shortly.

Stay close to the fence/wall on your right to reach a stile by the fence. Follow the fence round to the right, then go diagonally across the corner to reach a stile and yellow marker post. Go over the stile and ahead, then turn right across the drive and bear left following the arrow sign. Follow the path through the churchyard, around the back of the church to emerge onto the road.

10. Turn right, crossing the lane, and go into the field through the gate. Follow the direction of the footpath sign to walk with the hedge on your left for two fields. Go through a kissing gate and ahead on a path between hedges. At the far end go over a stile and continue ahead with a fence/hedge on your left. Go straight across the following field.

Note the old signal box to your right.

Go right down a short track and then bear left across the station yard.

To your left is the old Lowesby Station, which was on the Great Northern Line. The station opened in 1882 and closed to regular traffic in 1953.

On the far side of the yard, pass the small building to your left and go up the bank to a marker post and stile. Bear right, going onto a lane and up the hill. Continue past the buildings of Springfield Hill and go through the gate on the far side. Keep straight ahead in the next field. In the following field, go ahead bearing right around the hillock to reach a marker post in the right-hand corner.

11. Go through the gate and bear right to go behind the wire fencing and through a rickety gate at a marker post. Go left up a gully. When you see a marker post (hidden in the hedge on your left) bear right up the hill and head for another marker post before the houses. Go through a gate and onto a lane and ahead to reach Digby Close to return to the parking.

WALK 29
TILTON ON THE HILL 2
10 miles

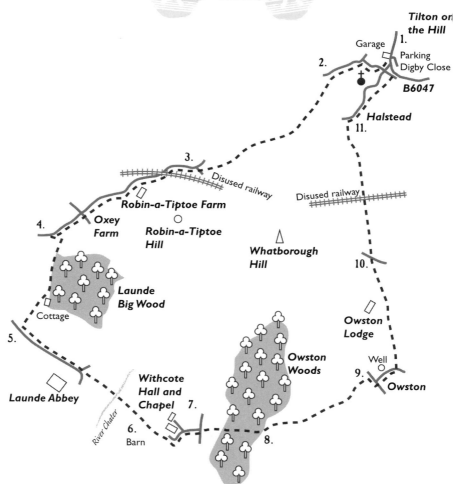

This is a second walk from the area known as High Leicestershire. It has excellent views and circles two of the highest hills in this part of Leicestershire. It is on paths, through fields and woods and quiet country lanes. An amusing legend and a visit to the beautiful 16th-century tiny chapel at Withcote Hall are an added bonus.

Distance: 10 miles
Grade: B/C
Parking: Digby Close, off Leicester Road (opposite Tilton Garage), Tilton on the Hill.
Map ref: SK 742057. Explorer 233 Leicester & Hinckley map.
Pub stop: None.

ROUTE -

1. Go out of Digby Close and turn left on Leicester Road. After 200 yards turn right on a road signposted Halstead and Loddington. Then turn right at the Rose and Crown, going onto Main Street. Turn left to walk through the churchyard and rejoin this road further down. When you come to a T-junction turn left, signposted Oxey and Loddington. Continue past the houses. Note there is the Old Beer House followed by Woodbine Cottage. Pass a footpath to the left, then turn left at the second footpath.

2. Go over the stile and follow the direction of the arrow, climbing up the field to reach a marker post and stile. Go slightly left in the second field. In the third field bear slightly right to a marker post by a gate (not the one in the corner). Keep straight ahead in the fourth field to a stile in the left-hand corner.

The hill to the left with the radio mast and reservoir on the top is Whatborough Hill. At 724ft, it is among the highest in Leicestershire and in mediaeval times had a village, now deserted, on its summit. The flat-topped hill straight ahead is Robin-a-Tiptoe.

Go straight across the next two fields and then bear right in the following two fields to reach a lane.

3. Turn left then take the right-hand fork. Stay on this quiet country lane, crossing and then walking beside an old disused railway.

This was part of the Great Northern and London NW Railway Joint Line, which ran from Market Harborough to Bottesford and Saxondale via Melton Mowbray and operated between 1879 and 1964. As well as passenger traffic, the line was used to transport iron ore, coal, grain and cattle and up to 8,000 gallons of milk per day.

In winter the fox-hunting season attracted the jet set of the time, who stayed in their lodges in the Melton area. They would send their mounts ahead by this line to the location of the meet. Special trains carried 20 to 30 horses to places such as Hallaton and Tilton, while their riders followed by carriage and in later years by motor car.

After ½ mile you reach the rather attractive sandstone building of the abandoned Robin-a-Tiptoe Farm on the left, with the flat top of the hill behind.

In olden days a gallows stood on the top of Robin-a-Tiptoe Hill. At that time it was called Howback Hill and the unfortunate felons hanged there would have been visible to all who passed by. Its later name is said to derive

Robin-a-Tiptoe Hill, the scene of an amusing legend.

from a sheep rustler called Robin who was extremely tall. When he was caught and hanged his toes just scraped the ground, taking a fraction of his weight. Whether this was just luck or lack of foresight on behalf of the hangman is not known, but when he was cut down later, he was able to be revived. He escaped any further punishment and the hill has been known as Robin-a-Tiptoe Hill ever since!

After another ½ mile you reach Oxey Farm and beyond it Oxey Cross Roads. Go straight over and continue for another ¼ mile.

4. Turn left at a footpath sign and yellow marker post. Go through the wooden gate and turn left to walk with the hedge on your left. At the corner follow it round to the right and continue up the field. At the top of this field go straight ahead for two large fields with Launde Big Wood to your left.

Launde Big Wood is one of the largest ancient woodlands in Leicestershire and Rutland.

The derelict cottage to the left of the second field has E.F.D. 1860 on the outside and a recipe for Yorkshire pudding scrawled on the wall inside!

After passing the cottage continue on a track to reach a road.

5. Turn left. Stay on this road for ½ mile, dropping down the hill and passing Launde Abbey on your right.

Launde Abbey is an Elizabethan manor house which was built on the site of an Augustinian priory. The original priory was founded in the early 12th century. Thomas Cromwell, Henry VIII's minister in charge of the Dissolution of the Monasteries, fell in love with its situation and wrote in his journal 'Myself for Launde'. However, he never occupied it as he was executed for treason in 1540, the year that building of the present house commenced. His son Gregory lived at Launde for 10 years with his wife Elizabeth, the sister of Jane Seymour, the third wife of Henry VIII.

When you reach the crossroads beyond the Abbey, go ahead over the cattle grid then leave the road heading for the telegraph pole. The path is not defined here and the marker post for the Leicestershire Round is wonky! Head for the highest point of the grassy hill on the horizon and the lowest of the telegraph poles below the hill, and finally you will pick up a marker post. Continue past the marker post, following its direction bearing left, dropping down to reach a stile and bridge over the River Chater. Go up the hill to another stile and yellow marker post and follow the direction of the arrow to the top of the hill.

The beautiful herd of horses which grazes on this hilltop belongs to Withcote Hall Stud, which has both stallions and brooding mares and is situated in the valley below.

From the top, go diagonally left down to the corner, passing the barn to your right.

6. Keep straight ahead on a track. As the track goes left, Withcote Hall comes into view. Go through a large gate and straight ahead and through a second double gate and continue on the paved farm track. At a road junction, go left to visit Withcote Chapel. This drive leads to the 18th-century Withcote Hall and you arrive in front of it, but there is public access to the chapel, which is open daily. Go past the Hall on your left, then turn right and then left to the chapel.

Withcote Chapel was built shortly after 1500 but was extensively remodelled inside in the 18th century and resembles a college chapel. Its beautiful stained-glass windows are comprised of 18 panels depicting eight apostles and 10 prophets. The glass dates back to 1530 and is said to be by

Withcote Chapel, one of Leicestershire's best-kept secrets.

Henry VIII's own glazier, Galeon Hone, but was moved to the chapel at a later date. This has to be one of Leicestershire's hidden gems and perhaps one of its best-kept secrets, judging by the lack of signage pointing to it. It is well worth spending a few peaceful minutes within its lovely walls.

7. Leaving the chapel, return down the drive and, at the junction, bear left through the electric gate. The button is on the right five yards before it and it closes automatically. Go up the lane to reach a main road. Go straight across, over the stile and up the hill and into Owston Woods. Go straight through the woods on a path which is muddy in places.

8. On the far side go over the stile and go diagonally left in the field to a marker post in the corner. In the following field continue in the same direction to a marker in the middle of the end hedge. Follow the direction of the arrow in field three, heading for a gap in the next hedge. In field four go straight ahead to a marker post by a five-bar gate. Follow the direction of the arrow in field five, bearing right to a marker post in the middle of the hedge, but do not go over the stile. Instead, turn left to keep the hedge on your right (this direction is not signed). At the bottom of the field, go through an iron gate (with a yellow sign) onto a green lane. Stay on this lane to reach another gate leading onto a road.

9. Turn right. Then, at the road junction, turn left, signposted 'Owston and Marefield'. This is the village of Owston. Note the old well in a field to the

Withcote Chapel interior – a hidden gem.

left. When you come to a footpath sign and yellow marker post, turn left through the small iron gate. Bear left to a yellow marker by a large iron gate. Go ahead on the path, passing a pond to your left, crossing a bridge and bearing right in the field. Go straight across field two then walk with the hedge on your right down field three, following it round to the left at the bottom to reach a stile and marker post. Pass another pond to your left and go straight up the hill. Continue across the next field and the drive and lawns of Owston Lodge and straight ahead in a final large field to reach a road.

10. Cross over and bear left. The pointed spire of Tilton on the Hill church may be seen on the horizon and is just to the right of your direction down the field. Cross the farm track and head diagonally left across the field to the corner. Go through the first gate and immediately left through a second, then turn right following the direction of the arrow sign. Drop down the field to a stile in the valley. Go up the steps to reach the old railway track you walked beside in the early part of the walk. At the top of the steps, turn left then almost immediately right at a marker post, dropping down and up some more steps. Go straight ahead in the field. On the far side of this enormous field, cross the corner of the next one and then continue with the hedge on your left. When you come to the farm go straight ahead on the gravelled lane, following it to the left and right and continuing until you reach a road.

11. Turn right. Note an old water pump opposite Halstead Grange. Just past a post box turn right at a footpath sign for Marefield Lane. Go through a kissing gate and ahead with a hedge on your left for three fields. Go through an iron kissing gate and ahead between fence and hedge to reach a road. Turn left, then at the Rose and Crown pub turn right. Turn left at the Leicester Road and right on Digby Close to the parking.

WALK 30
HUNGARTON
9½ miles

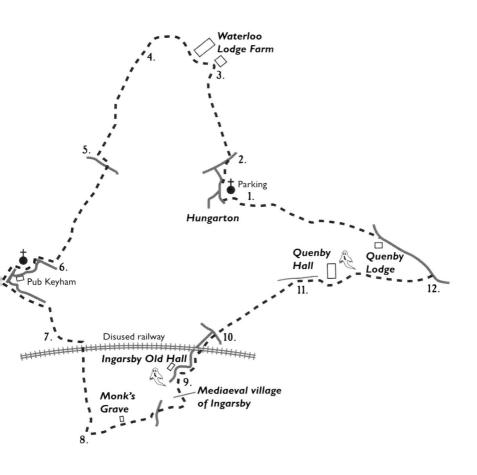

This is the third of the walks in High Leicestershire. Like the others it has excellent views, a variety of scenery and a wealth of interest. It is mostly on good paths, tracks and lanes with some field walking. Sprayed paths have been left through the crop fields but others have been left as meadowland and are more overgrown. The bonus is that they are covered in wildflowers in late spring and summer.

Distance: 9½ miles

Grade: B

Parking: Limited parking is available on Church Lane off Main Street, Hungarton.

Map ref: SK 691073. Explorer 233 Leicester & Hinckley Map.

Pub stop: Dog and Gun pub, Keyham. Open 12–3pm daily, except Mondays.

ROUTE

1. From Church Lane return to Main Street and turn right. Go up the road as it winds right and left, then opposite Jasmine Cottage and a footpath sign, go right over a gravelled area. Then, after 30 yards, go left through a kissing gate and diagonally across the field. Go through an iron kissing gate onto the road and turn right.

2. After 100 yards, turn left at a marker post and go diagonally right across the corner of the field to a stile in the middle of the hedge. Cross a private road and follow the direction of the arrow in the next field to reach a marker post, turning left to a stile. In the next field go straight ahead with the fence on your left. At the end of the fence, bear right to a marker post in the far hedge. In the next field keep straight ahead, then in the following field bear left to a marker post in front of the big barn.

3. Go through a five-bar gate and ahead in the field with the hedge on your right. At the next marker post, go through the gate and go diagonally right in the field to a marker post in the far corner. Pass through a gateway and turn left, then through a five-bar gate and straight ahead with a hedge on your left. At the end of the hedge, continue in the same direction for the remainder of the field.

4. Go through the gate and turn left (this direction is not signed), to walk down the field with the hedge on your left. Bear diagonally left across a green lane and continue in the next field now with the hedge on your right. At the end of this large and rather boring field, cross a bridge in the corner and keep straight ahead for the next two fields. At the end of the second field, go over a stile and ahead with a hedge on your right to reach a road.

5. Turn left. After 300 yards turn right at a public bridleway sign and go down two fields with the hedge on your right. At the bottom of the second field, follow the hedge round to the left to reach a marker post. Cross the bridge and go up the next field with the hedge on your left to reach a road. Cross over and go over the stile and follow the direction of the arrow across the field. Go through three gates to reach the road.

6. Turn right and then turn left on King's Lane and right on Main Street into Keyham.

All Saints' Church provides a seat for a break or, if preferred, the Dog and Gun pub further down the village is open 12–3pm every day except Monday.

Continue down Main Street to reach a T junction (just beyond the pub). Turn left and stay on the road beyond the houses where it becomes a lane. Keep straight ahead at Keyham Kennels and Cattery, following a bridleway sign hidden in the hedge. Cross the yard and go through the gateway on the far side and ahead on a broad path between a wood and a hedge. Then, in the field beyond, walk between a fence and a hedge.

7. In the next field, turn left and go up the field on a broad track. At the end of the field, at a marker post, turn right to go up the adjoining field with the hedge on your right. Go through a gate and ahead between the walls of the old railway which ran from Leicester. Cross the next two fields with a hedge on your right. Then keep straight ahead in the third and fourth fields.

8. Go left on a broad track. Go through an open gateway and continue on the track with a fence on your right. Pass through a second gateway. Then, after 200 yards, note the nettle-covered mound to your left.

This moated mound is known as the Monk's Grave, but is actually a motte and bailey castle dating back to the reign of King Stephen (1135–54).

Stay on the track as it drops down the hill.

In the field ahead, on the horizon, the ridges, furrows and squares of the mediaeval village of Ingarsby may be seen outlined in the grass.

At the bottom of the hill, go through the gate onto the lane. Turn left, then, after 100 yards, turn right through a gate at a bridleway sign.

The mediaeval village of Ingarsby was sited in the field ahead of you, and you can see the holloway up the middle which formed the main street, and the mounds of house platforms. It was originally a Danish settlement founded around the ninth century, which had grown substantially by Norman times. However, in the middle of the 15th century the land was owned by the Canons of Leicester Abbey and they decided that, as the price of wool was rising, sheep were more profitable than people. Consequently the villagers were thrown out and the land turned to pasture.

The path up this field is unclear due to the lumps and hollows of the village. Follow the direction of the bridleway sign from the gate then, when you reach the highest point of the field with a fence ahead, go left towards the buildings of Ingarsby Old Hall to reach a gate onto a road.

9. Turn right and go past Ingarsby Old Hall.

Ingarsby Old Hall is a moated manor house. Most of it dates from the 17th century, but one part, known as 'the Chapel', is the 15th-century grange of Leicester Abbey. In 1439, Abbot Sadyngton was investigating the theft of silver plate from the Chapel. When he had no success with normal methods it seems he was not averse to resorting to the occult. It is reported that he smeared the thumbnail of a local boy named Maurice with oil and told him to describe what he saw there, while the Abbot chanted charms. The boy duly said that he saw Thomas Asty, the Canon of Ingarsby Chapel, taking the silver plate. When the Canon was arrested, he confessed to the theft and the plate was recovered.

Stay on the road as it winds right and left. Go through a bridge under the old railway track you crossed earlier and continue to a main road.

Ingarsby Old Hall, where sorcery was used to catch a thief.

10. Turn right and almost immediately left at a public bridleway sign. Go down the first field and straight ahead in fields two and three to a gate in the corner. Bear right in the fourth field, heading for a five-bar gate and marker post which comes into view, situated 50 yards to the right of a brick bridge. Bear left from the gate to reach the drive of Quenby Hall.

Note the ridge and furrow pattern left by mediaeval ploughing in the field to the right. The up and down ploughing of long strips with a particular type of plough threw the soil towards the centre of the strip, producing a high ridge. It was in this area that the mediaeval village of Quenby once stood.

11. Turn right on the drive and continue towards the Hall.

This magnificent Jacobean house was built in 1627 and remained in the Ashby family for 300 years. It is now owned by the De Lisle family, whose ancestry can be traced back to the Norman Conquest.

There are reports of many strange happenings over the years. A ghostly lady has been seen walking the landing and down the stairs. In one of the rooms, a member of staff heard a clock chime 12 even though it was never wound and the time was incorrect.

Several people witnessed the top from a decanter popping out and flying across the room one evening. Another member of staff heard a noise behind her and saw that a stool had moved and was wedging the door closed. Scratches have been heard coming from a velvet headboard and a grey lady has been seen walking from the parlour to the library.

Outside a ghostly white horse may be seen galloping across the valley.

Quenby Hall has another claim to fame. It is where Stilton cheese was first made by the housekeeper and sold by her daughter at a staging inn at Stilton.

Just before the Hall, bear right to reach a small gate with a yellow-topped post. Go straight ahead with a wall to your left.

Quenby is home to an organic herd of about 150 English Longhorn cattle, named for their typically long, down-curving horns. The English Longhorn is regarded as the oldest pure breed of cattle in England. Though they look rather formidable, I found them fine as long as I gave them a wide berth, particularly where there were calves. However, be warned — they do seem to suddenly panic and charge across the field to be all together. In this case just stand still and let them go.

And beware of the ghostly white horse galloping about too.

Quenby Hall, where there are reports of many strange happenings.

Where the wall ends, bear left to a marker post and turn right on the track. Stay on this track, passing through three gates to reach a road.

12. Turn left. Stay on this road for ½ mile then, just past the buildings of Quenby Lodge, turn left at a footpath sign. Bear right across the corner of the field. In the second field walk with the hedge on your right, then go straight across the third field. Go over the stile and straight ahead to a marker post and bridge hidden in the hedge. Cross the bridge and a stile and then turn right to walk with the hedge on your right.

In the following field, keep the hedge on your left until you reach a marker post just past a five-bar gate, then turn left over a bridge and stile. Turn right to walk with the hedge on your right. Go through a gate and pass a wood on your right. Then, at the end of the field, go between iron rails and up a narrow path to reach a small gate onto a lane. Turn left and continue back on to Church Lane.

BIBLIOGRAPHY

Bell, David *Leicestershire and Rutland Ghosts & Legends* David Bell, 2001.

Black, Annis *Leicestershire Legends* Heart of Albion Press, 2004.

Bourne, Jill *Understanding Leicestershire & Rutland Place Names* Heart of Albion Press, 2003.

Wright, Andrew James *Ghosts and Hauntings in and around Leicestershire* Heart of Albion Press, 2006.

INDEX